ASTON MARTIN

SINCE **1994**

First published in April 2008

A catalogue record for this book is available from the British Library

ISBN 978 1 84425 445 3

Library of Congress control no. 2007943090

Published by Haynes Publishing,
Sparkford, Yeovil, Somerset BA22 7JJ, UK.
Tel: 01963 442030 Fax: 01963 440001
Int. tel: +44 1963 442030
Int. fax: +44 1963 440001
E-mail: sales@haynes.co.uk
Website: www.haynes.co.uk

Haynes North America Inc., 861 Lawrence Drive,
Newbury Park, California 91320, USA

Design and layout by Richard Parsons

Printed and bound in Britain by J. H. Haynes & Co. Ltd,
Sparkford, Yeovil, Somerset BA22 7JJ

AUTOCAR
COLLECTION
ASTON MARTIN
SINCE **1994**

Haynes Publishing

CONTENTS

Autocar Collection: Aston Martin since 1994

The best words, photos and data from the world's oldest car magazine

INTRODUCTION

Chas Hallett
Editor, Autocar

As the world's oldest motoring magazine, *Autocar* has driven and written about virtually every Aston Martin model ever built. By the time the marque started life in 1914 we were already nearly 20 years old. Our stories of the time show that Aston began life the way it has continued, as an icon of performance, technical excellence and exclusivity.

However the Aston models launched since 1994, which are covered in this collection of *Autocar* features, are the most important it has ever published on the marque, for two important reasons. First, they show how Aston's modern era began with the launch of the DB7, which will always be one of the marque's most influential and important cars. It founded a new design style for Astons, and took sales volume from a few dozen a year into the thousands. It also re-established Aston as a fast-car name that could be uttered in the same breath as Porsche or Ferrari, a highly significant development.

The Aston Martin DB7 also provided the secure foundation from which the Vanquish was developed, and that last-ever Newport Pagnell model went on to pioneer the construction technology that underpins today's Astons. The combined success of both cars gave the company the confidence to begin its 'Gaydon era' in 2003, and since then the company has launched the increasingly successful DB9 and V8 Vantage models, both built in one of the world's most progressive fast-car factories..

Today, Aston Martin makes more road cars annually than Ferrari, and earns very impressive profits, a key ability that eluded it for fully 90 years, and the future looks brighter than ever. In sum, this book is a story of boldness, design and engineering excellence and class-beating creativity, all seen through the eyes of *Autocar*'s road testers and photographers. It is a unique insight, and we hope you enjoy it.

ASTON MARTIN DB7

Aston has waited a long time for a car that offers performance, sophistication and pedigree at a realistic price. Now the waiting is over

The bottom line is this: the fragile future of Britain's most distinguished marque is in the hands of this car, the Aston Martin DB7. Succeed and the old firm will build more cars and make more money than at any time in its heroically troubled 75 years. Fail and few would bet on its parent, Ford, finding the patience and money to fund an all-new replacement. The gates at Newport Pagnell could just shut for good.

Not, you understand, that the DB7 is built at Newport Pagnell or, as the accompanying panel overleaf makes clear, was even conceived there. By the end of the year, 150 DB7s will have rolled out of a factory near Bloxham, Oxfordshire, where the last tenant was the Jaguar XJ220. Next year, Aston Martin aims to raise that figure to 700, or four times its annual sales of late. It costs £78,500 and, for now, there are no Vantage of Volante versions, although rumours of both abound.

If looks alone determined success then the bosses at Aston Martin would sleep soundly. Its shape has a beauty the motoring world is lucky to see once in a generation. The last time the UK produced a sporting car of such beauty, Jaguar called it the E-type.

QUICK FACTS

Model	Aston Martin DB7
Price	£78,500
Top speed	157mph
0–60mph	5.8sec
30–70mph	5.4sec
MPG	17.1
For	Classic bodywork, ride quality, lusty engine, fine handling, beautiful finish, sumptuous cabin
Against	Too much wind noise, driveline shunt, panel fit, facia layout, small boot

Its brief is simply to be the finest Grand Tourer available for a five figure sum. Simple, that is, if you don't regard the likes of the BMW 850CSi, Mercedes S500C and Jaguar XJS V12 as serious competition.

PERFORMANCE ★★★★

The engine of an Aston Martin is its heart as surely as it is a Ferrari's. For the DB7, Aston Martin has forsaken the big V8 that has been its mainstay for the past 20 years and invoked a still older tradition by installing a twin-cam straight six, the sort of engine that powered all DBs from two to six.

Relieved of the V8's bulk, Aston Martin nevertheless needed its power and throttle response and therefore called upon the services of an intercooled Eaton supercharger blowing at one atmosphere through the 3239cc, 24-valve all-aluminium six. The result is a power peak of 335bhp at 5500rpm and a thunderous 360lb ft of torque at 3000rpm, both enough to overshadow Aston's stock 5.3-litre V8.

Harness this power to a body that uses lightweight composites to create a kerb weight of just 1750kg, giving a power-to-weight ratio of 191bhp per tonne, and it's easy to see how the DB7's impressive headline performance figures are achieved. Any car that can reach 60mph from rest in 5.8sec, break the 100mph barrier just 8.6sec later and crack 157mph is clearly extremely swift but this is, in fact, the poorest measure of the DB7's performance. Because the supercharger is driven directly by the engine, not the exhaust like a turbo, there is no delay between your request for power and its arrival.

And then there's the noise. At low revs and modest throttle inputs, the engine warbles a slightly uneven yet enchanting burr that's more reminiscent of a Volvo or Audi five-cylinder engine than a British six. But open the throttles wide and the deep thrum is overlaid by a fascinating supercharger whine that's more akin to a pre-war racing car than a modern GT.

ROAD TEST

19 OCTOBER 1994

Volume 202

No 3 | 5098

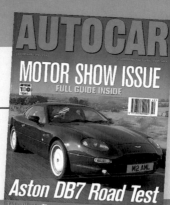

AUTOCAR

MOTOR SHOW ISSUE
FULL GUIDE INSIDE

Aston DB7 Road Test

This Week: Three New Ferraris New Audi 80 Drive
New Caterham Mansell New Ford Probe First Pics

ABOVE Steering wheel adjusts for rake only, not enough for huge motorised seats to achieve ideal driving position.

If only the remainder of the driveline set such sublime standards. It doesn't. Most disappointing in a car with such a sophisticated brief is the degree of slack and shunt in the driveline, which makes achieving a truly clean getaway something of a conjuring trick.

HYBRID TO WELL BRED IN THREE

It's no coincidence that the DB7 shares engine and suspension designs with the Jaguar XJS. Deep, deep in its history, it is an XJS, but let's get one thing straight: none of that matters, any more than it matters that a McLaren F1 V12 is made from two BMW M3 engines, or an XJ220 uses an engine that started life in a Metro. The DB7's character, its manner, its ability, all come from Tom Walkinshaw's engineering.

We do know that a project existed at TWR in 1991 called 'XX'. Commissioned by Ford, it gave Jaguar an image car via the expedient method of grafting a body with more than a passing resemblance to the stillborn XJ41 F-type. Nothing much was heard of it until June 1992, when Aston Martin announced the formation of Aston Martin Oxford Ltd to build an £80,000 coupé codenamed, get this NPX. The NP stood for Newport Pagnell.

What's more, the announcement revealed that prototypes had been up and running for six months, presumably as XXs.

Aston Martin has never commented on the DB7's tortured genesis and nor need it. It only knows how badly it needed NPX, Jag-based or not.

Nor is the five-speed manual gearbox a patch on the engine it regulates (four electronically controlled automatic gears are available for no extra charge). Like the clutch, it is quite heavy, while the throws between the ratios are slow and not particularly enjoyable. Mercifully, the engine covers well for its comparatively underachieving transmission, providing torque in such quantities from any speed above idle that gearchanging is kept to a minimum.

ECONOMY ★★★

One of the claims made by detractors of the supercharger is that it makes an engine too thirsty. In this respect, however, the Aston acquitted itself tolerably, returning an average of 17.1mpg in our hands. A light foot will realise up to 26mpg, while routine consumption should never sink below 15mpg.

The fuel tank holds an impressive 88.5 litres (19.5 gallons), but our test car's tendency to blink its fuel warning light after consuming just 60 litres effectively reduced its potential range from 500 miles to a rather disappointing 300 miles.

HANDLING ★★★★

The DB7 has a chassis of rare quality and, as you will read in the ride section, this does not merely manifest itself in corners and curves. In such circumstances, however, the DB7 is in its element. Too many GTs become flustered or anaesthetised on challenging roads, but the DB7 attacks them like a starving man at a pie-eating contest.

Its suspension may follow the traditional Jaguar route of double wishbones at the front with a lower wishbone and driveshafts acting as upper links at the back, but the Trojan efforts of Tom Walkinshaw's development team have paid off.

Chunky, but not excessive 245.40 section Bridgestone tyres clothe mighty 18in wheels and generate a level of dry road grip that is phenomenal for a front-engined coupé designed primarily for touring. Whether you want unflinching lateral adhesion or the traction to allow you to tread hard at the apex of a right corner with confidence, the DB7 delivers. Point it at a road full of crests and dips, off-camber corners and hidden turns and the Aston will wolf it down without scraping its belly, floating or wobbling.

Ultimately, it will push its tail wide if you are too liberal with the power in a corner, especially it if is wet and, once the back starts to move, it does so quite quickly. Nevertheless, it still slides progressively and cleanly and requires no more than a twist of the wheel to set the car straight again.

The steering itself is less accomplished. In its defence the weighting is perfect, the wheel feels delightful in your hands and it is unlikely that many DB7s will have to park in tight urban streets or supermarket car parks so the poor lock may not matter too much. However, it turns the Aston into corners a shade too aggressively and possesses insufficient feel to do justice to the messages coming through the chassis.

RIDE ★★★★★

Styling aside, this is the DB7's greatest achievement. The balance it strikes back-lane body control is so delicate it makes the efforts of even such vaunted chassis wizards as BMW look a little gauche.

Paper-thin tyre sidewalls barely make an impression on the Aston's ability to soak up potholes, while iron-willed damping confers a stability over motorway undulations that many all-out luxury saloons would do well to emulate.

ROAD TEST DB7

ACCELERATION FROM REST

True mph	seconds	speedo mph
30	2.2	32
40	3.3	44
50	4.5	54
60	5.8	65
70	7.6	76
80	9.4	86
90	11.5	96
100	14.4	106
110	17.5	116
120	21.0	127
130	26.3	137

Standing qtr mile 14.3sec/100mph
Standing km 25.8sec/130mph
30–70mph through the gears 5.4sec

ACCELERATION IN GEAR

MPH	5th	4th	3rd	2nd
10–30	-	7.0	4.4	2.7
20–40	8.8	5.6	3.6	2.4
30–50	7.9	5.0	3.2	2.4
40–60	7.3	4.7	3.3	2.5
50–70	7.1	4.6	3.6	-
60–80	7.1	4.8	3.6	-
70–90	7.2	5.3	3.9	-
80–100	7.8	5.7	-	-
90–110	9.1	5.9	-	-
100–120	10.6	7.1	-	-
110–120	12.2	-	-	-
120–140	14.3	-	-	-

MAXIMUM SPEEDS

5th	157mph/5500rpm	4th	130/6000
3rd	92/6000	2nd	66/6000
1st	37/6000		

CONSUMPTION

Average/best/worst/touring
17.1/26.2/9.7/26.2mpg

Urban	15.5mpg
56mph	32.8mpg
75mph	25.8mpg
Tank capacity	88.5 litres
Touring range	510 miles

BRAKES

30/50/70mph   9.3/26.5/51.4 metres

NOISE

Idle/max revs in 3rd 51/82dbA
30/50/70mph 55/65/75dbA

TESTER'S NOTES

- The view out over that extraordinary bonnet, the supercharger scream, the quality of the interior materials, the dinner plate alloys.

- The position of cruise control switches, lack of an airbag, fiddly stereo controls, poor steering lock, lack of steering reach control, cheap wiper stalks.

ASTON MARTIN DB7 AND ITS RIVALS

MAKE	ASTON MARTIN	BMW	MERCEDES-BENZ	PORSCHE
Model	**DB7**	**850 CSi**	**S500 C**	**928 GTS**
Price	£78,500	£79,750	£74,600	£72,950
Capacity	3239cc	5576cc	4973cc	5397mm
Power	335bhp at 5500rpm	380bhp at 5300rpm	304bhp at 5500rpm	350bhp at 5700rpm
Torque	360lb ft at 3000rpm	405lb ft at 4000rpm	347lb ft at 3900rpm	362lb ft at 4250rpm
Max speed	157mph	155mph	153mph	168mph
0–60mph	5.8sec	5.9sec	7.9sec	5.4sec
30–70mph through gears	5.4sec	5.0sec	6.8sec	4.9sec
Standing quarter mile	14.3sec	14.4sec	16.1sec	14.1sec
30–50mph in 4th	5.0sec	5.1sec	2.8sec	4.1sec
50–70mph in top	7.1sec	8.8sec	4.0sec	5.9sec
Mpg overall/touring	17.1/26.2	15.1/20.9	17.2/23.7	14.8/19.9
Mph/1000rpm in top	28.6	30.1	28.1	26.5
Kerb weight	1750kg	1950kg	2070kg	1600kg
Date tested	19.10.94	n/a	24.8.94	23.9.92
VERDICT	★★★★	★★★	★★★	★★★

WHAT IT COSTS

ASTON MARTIN DB7

List price	£78,500
Total as tested	£79,323
Cost per mile	na

INSURANCE

Insurance/typical quote	20/na

WARRANTY

12 months unlimited mileage, anti-corrosion protection and recovery service

SERVICING

3.2-hour service every 7500 miles

PARTS PRICES

Tyre (each, typical)	£275.00
Other parts prices to be announced	

EQUIPMENT CHECKLIST

Automatic transmission	nco
Metallic paint	■
Seatbelt pre-tensioners	-
Alarm with immobiliser	■
Electrically adjusted mirrors	■
Electric windows	■
Heated seats	■
RDS radio/cassette	■
10 CD autochanger	**£823**
Leather upholstery	■
Anti-lock brakes	■
Air conditioning	■
Driver's seat lumbar adjustment	-
Adjustable steering column	■
Cruise control	■
Heated windscreen	■

Options in **bold** fitted to test car
■ = Standard na = not available

But it is on A and B-roads that the Aston's talents really shine and the secret to its cross-county pace is revealed: so well does it resist body roll and refuse to throw its passengers around the cabin that the DB7 is able to maintain a pace that would prove uncomfortable and even unnerving in a lesser car.

BRAKES ★★

We don't doubt the DB7's ability to stop swiftly in a straight line when asked, but that should be the starting point for a modern car. When you are paying close to £80,000 for a sporting tourer, you have a right to expect a sponge-free and progressive pedal and here the DB7 falls down badly. Although it is easy to slow the car smoothly at urban speeds, judging comfortable barking distances and shedding speed consistently on faster roads is altogether more tricky. Also, the standard anti-lock of the test car would occasionally be fooled into operation under braking at only moderate effort over a crest.

AT THE WHEEL ★★★

There's a lot to find fault with here. For such a quintessentially British car, the driving position is distinctly Italian, offering insufficient room for your right leg and a steering wheel that only adjusts for rake when it really needs reach control. In addition, the rim of the steering wheel conceals the outer edges of the ancillary instruments, which are themselves more attractive than readable.

The fat column stalks work well, as do the majority of minor switches, laid out in a neat and logical line across the centre console. Why Aston Martin then chose to locate the arm and cancel switches for the cruise control behind the gear lever is beyond us. But all-round visibility is impressive

ABOVE LEFT
Nowhere is DB7's dynamic excellence more evident than in its unbeatable ride quality; steering lags behind chassis, though, lacking its finesse in turn-in.

BELOW Boot small but usable.

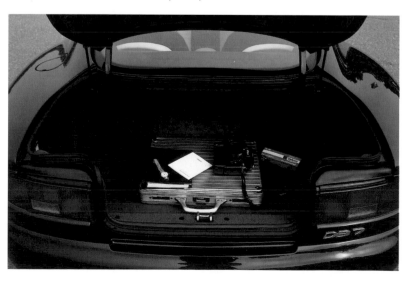

SPECIFICATIONS DB7

DIMENSIONS

Min/max front legroom 910/1100mm Max front headroom 900mm
Min/max rear legroom 410/600mm Max rear headroom 800mm
Min/max boot width 1050/1420mm Boot volume 0.17cu m Kerb weight 1750kg
Front/rear tracks 1524/1530mm Max payload 550kg Overall width 1820mm

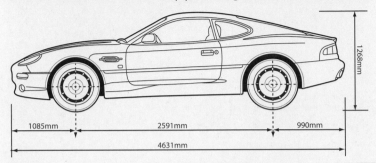

1085mm 2591mm 990mm
4631mm
1268mm

ENGINE

Layout	6 cyls in line, 3239cc
Max power	335bhp at 5500rpm
Max torque	360lb ft at 3000rpm
Specific output	103bhp per litre
Power to weight	191bhp per tonne
Torque to weight	206lb ft per tonne
Installation	longitudinal, front, rear-wheel drive
Construction	Alloy head and block
Bore/stroke	91mm/83mm
Valve gear	4 per cyl, dohc
Compression ratio	8.3:1
Ignition and fuel	Electronic ignition, Zytec multi-point sequential fuel injection, supercharger, intercooler

TRANSMISSION

Gearbox 5-speed manual
Ratios/mph per 1000rpm
Final drive ratio 3.54

1st	3.55/6.1	2nd	2.04/10.6
3rd	1.40/15.4	4th	1.00/21.6
5th	0.75/28.6		

STEERING

Type Rack and pinion, power assisted
Turns lock-to-lock 2.7
Turning circle 12.3m

CHASSIS AND BODY

Body	Two-door coupé
Wheels	8x18in
Made of	Cast alloy
Tyres	245/40 ZR18 Bridgestone Expedia
Spare	Space saver

SUSPENSION

Front double wishbones, coil springs, anti-roll bar
Rear lower wishbones with driveshaft acting as upper links, coil springs, anti-roll bar

BRAKES

Front 285mm ventilated discs
Rear 295mm plain discs
Anti-lock Standard

given the car's steeply raked lines and at least the air conditioning system offers a brilliant contrast of cold faces and warm feet to all those deft enough to master its over-sensitive operation.

ACCOMMODATION & COMFORT ★★★

By and large, cars in this class are pretty disgracefully packaged. Look in the back of a BMW 8-series, Jaguar XJS or Porsche 928 and you'll see what we mean. Those that offer meaningful space to rear seat occupants tend to do so at the expense of elegance, as demonstrated by the Mercedes S-class coupé.

No one would question the DB7's elegance, but nor would they call its rear cabin room generous. The truth is no adult will complete a journey in the back of a DB7 in anything less than acute discomfort. Many won't be able to climb into the deeply dished buckets at all. Forget teenagers and indeed anyone who finds short trousers embarrassing. Toddlers and small children will be able to live in the lack of head and legroom, but even they might find that having no visual stimulus beyond the unrelenting expanse of a seatback somewhat provocative.

The DB7 works much more successfully for two adults, with sufficient headroom for even the unusually tall and enough rearward travel for the passenger seat to allow your companion to stretch out. The seats themselves look huge in the Aston's cabin and come generously bolstered. Testers commented, however, that despite electric control, there was neither height nor tilt control while others reckoned the lumbar support met your back too high up the spine.

The boot is rather small and shallow by class standards, but should suffice for two on an informal holiday.

NOISE ★★

The DB7 has a big problem and Aston Martin knows it. By deciding early in the car's development to use the same system employed by BMW coupés of dropping the windows a fraction when the frameless doors are opened to equalise pressure when they shut, Aston Martin has bought in a level of wind noise that is totally at odds with the DB7's sophistication.

The first time you hear it, and in the test car it came on like a light switch at 60mph, you'll think you left a window open. At a cruise it is enough to make you question the DB7's grand touring credentials.

Aston claims that by the time cars reach customers the problem will have been addressed.

Otherwise the suppression of noise, especially from those fat tyres, is impressive. The engine only intrudes when you want it to and the suspension is admirably quiet. The only quibble is a body boom, most noticeable in top at about 1800rpm, which vanishes before 2000rpm.

BUILD QUALITY & SAFETY ★★★

The DB7 is painted by Rolls-Royce and comes with a finish that's equal to any car we have seen this year, McLaren F1 included. Inside, the quality of the materials from wood to leather to carpets is commensurate with a car of the price. But the way the DB7 is constructed leaves rather more to be desired. In particular, panel gaps are unfashionably wide and the doors sound tinny.

Although the DB7 has side-impact bars and anti-lock brakes as standard, airbags won't be available until next year, a bad omission in a luxury car costing £80,000.

EQUIPMENT & VALUE ★★★★

All the essentials are there, from leather to air conditioning, although we were surprised to see the CD stacker came from the options list.

If the finest materials wrapped in a beautiful shape are more important to you than gadgets, you will have little problem convincing yourself of its value.

ABOVE Front wishbones and 245/40 tyres combine to give Aston immense poise under pressure; throw it at a bend and it takes determination to budge the tail.

AUTOCAR VERDICT ★★★★

Even without the emotional knee-jerk reaction to a car of such beauty, the DB7 is a triumph. In nigh-on every area of engine and chassis performance it has what it takes to hold its own against the opposition and, in many spheres, shows them the way home.

Yet it feels unfinished. There are too many rough edges, particularly in the driveline, panel fit and noise suppression, which conspire to deny it the five-star verdict its talents seem to deserve.

These faults notwithstanding, the DB7 does enough to make it our runaway choice from its selected rivals, joining the McLaren F1 in re-establishing Britain at the cutting edge of specialist car making. The gates at Newport Pagnell should stay open for a while yet.

DB7 VOLANTE

Some will say that cutting the roof off one of the world's most beautiful cars is nothing short of criminal. But that is exactly what Aston Martin has done to the DB7

This car has many questions to answer if it is to justify the spectacular £89,950 asking price. Since the original DB7 went on sale, several changes have taken place to eradicate the glitches we highlighted back in October 1994.

Then, we applauded the spirit and ability of the DB7 but criticised its poor build quality and finish. This is an opportunity to put that memory to rest.

DESIGN AND ENGINEERING ★★★
Beautifully crafted, but detail design not as well thought out as a Jag or Merc

Perfectly timed to steal some thunder from Jaguar's new XK8 twins, the soft top DB7 Volante has taken two years longer to reach us than its beautiful fixed head sibling.

That's a long time to spend chopping the roof off. But, since the Volante marks Aston Martin's return to the critical quality US market – where it will cost almost 40 per cent more than the Mercedes SL500 – the Bloxham-based engineers have also taken the opportunity to thoroughly reappraise every aspect of the DB7. Although most of the updates are invisible, more than 600 new components have been developed for the Volante – over 200 of which are now also fitted to the improved coupé.

QUICK FACTS

Model	DB7 Volante
Price	£89,950
Top speed	152mph
30–70mph	6.4sec
0–60mph	6.5sec
60–0mph	2.8sec
For	Great handling and ride, looks, interior changes
Against	Engine not as good as XK8, fiddly hood, price

ROAD TEST

6 NOVEMBER 1996

Volume 210

No 6 | 5203

AUT⊙CAR

SCOOP! New Baby
Range Rover
Plus
100
secret
new
cars
for '97

Test: DB7 Volante
Tour of Britain by Ka
V6 test: 406 vs Mondeo
BMW 728i: 10,000 mile test

SPECIAL
AWARDS
ISSUE
TOP USED CARS:
BEST CHOICE

ABOVE Handsome lines remain, but hood stands too tall.

BELOW Reminders of the car's pedigree are everywhere.

To replace some of the torsional rigidity lost in deleting the coupé's roof, numerous tubular reinforcements, crossbraces and gussets have been added to its pressed steel structure. And the suspension on all Volantes has been softened, according to Aston, to suit American tastes. As a result, scuttle shake, if present, is well camouflaged.

Externally, the Volante is identical to the coupé apart from its new rear wings and boot lid, which are flatter and only slightly less voluptuous. But the purity of the body is spoiled by the clumsy powered roof, which nestles under an ugly, manually fitted, tonneau cover when folded. Aston says it considered a fully automatic, flush folding design, but abandoned it to maximise golf bag space in the boot.

Still, top up, the Volante looks great, and the snug-fitting soft top is fitted with a heated glass window.

Overall finish is fautless, with exquisite leather work, ultra tight panel gaps and peerless glassfibre body panels. It's just a pity that the Ford family parts bin switches, internal door handles and hood catches don't quite live up to the price tag.

PERFORMANCE AND BRAKES ★★★
Disappointing performance, slower than a 500SL, less musical than an XK8

Under the still gorgeous bonnet of the Volante, lies the same Eaton supercharged 3239cc straight six cylinder engine from the coupé. It has a new Ford EEC V engine management chip, but still produces 335bhp at 5750rpm and 361lb ft of torque at just 3000rpm. However, compared with the coupé, its performance is significantly blunted.

The Volante is 50kg heavier than the DB7 that *Autocar* first tested. But, according to those at Newport Pagnell, the difference is smaller now, since the coupé has put on weight since 1994, with the addition of airbags and other modifications.

As a result, this five-speed manual car cracks the 60mph barrier in 6.5 seconds, seven tenths of a second slower than the coupé, and only slightly faster than Jaguar's claimed 6.7 seconds for the automatic XK8 convertible. It's also surprising that nearly £90,000 doesn't buy you traction control.

Through the gears between 30mph and 70mph, the clock ticks for 6.4 seconds, a full second longer than it takes the coupé, and 1.2 seconds slower than a Mercedes 500SL. And in top, 50–70mph takes 8.2 seconds, before the car reaches its 153mph top speed. It's a slightly disappointing performance and, welcome as the familiar whine of the supercharger is, it doesn't match the cultured sound of an XK8.

If it was our money, we'd forego a little performance and have an automatic gearbox. The manual has a very heavy clutch and, although the shift is quite good, it takes concentration to perfect gearchanges.

The brakes, however, offer reassuring, powerful and progressive performance. That nearly two tonnes of metal can be stopped from 60mph to a standstill in just 2.8 seconds is all the proof you need.

HANDLING AND RIDE ★★★★
Stiffer than an SL, hardly any scuttle shake, confidence-inspiring handling

Aston has achieved wonders here. It always claimed the DB7 Volante was conceived alongside the coupé, but doubters didn't believe it. It's time to start believing.

Nobody would expect the Volante to outhandle or outride the coupé, but it gets much closer than you'd imagine. The first surprise comes along a rippled B road where the DB7 feels more rigid than the benchmark Mercedes SL. Its composure remains even when the road deteriorates, and only serious bumps reveal a small amount of chassi flex. In more typical situations, the ride from the independent double wishbone suspension is absorbent but firm, displaying a confidence rarely found in cars of this type. In town it rides with impressive bump control; but on motorways, although the ride is comfortable over some surfaces a vibration through the steering column becomes noticeable.

ROAD TEST DB7 VOLANTE

ACCELERATION FROM REST

True mph	seconds	speedo mph
30	2.4	31
40	3.6	43
50	5.0	54
60	6.5	64
70	8.8	75
80	11.1	85
90	13.8	94
100	17.6	103
110	21.9	112
120	27.5	120

Standing qtr mile 15.2sec/94mph
Standing km 27.3sec/120mph
30–70mph through gears 6.4sec

ACCELERATION IN GEAR

MPH	5th	4th	3rd	2nd
10–30	-	-	5.0	3.0
20–40	10.3	6.4	4.0	2.6
30–50	9.1	5.8	3.8	2.6
40–60	8.5	5.6	4.2	3.0
50–70	8.2	5.7	3.6	-
60–80	8.2	4.7	3.6	-
70–90	8.1	4.8	5.0	-
70–90	8.1	4.8	5.0	-
80–100	8.7	6.4	-	-
90–110	9.8	6.7	-	-
100–120	15.1	8.5	-	-

MAXIMUM SPEEDS

5th 152mph/5500rpm	4th 136/6500
3rd 97/6500	2nd 66/6500
1st 38/6500	

FUEL CONSUMPTION

Average/best/worst/touring
18.5/26.3/11.2/26.3mpg

Urban	32.8mpg
Extra urban	25.8mpg
Combined	15.5mpg
Tank capacity	89 litres
Touring range	515 miles

BRAKES

30/50/70mph	11.1/27.3/52.2 metres
60–0mph	3.2sec

NOISE

Idle/max revs in 3rd 50/77dbA
30/50/70mph 61/63/69dbA

SPECIFICATIONS DB7 VOLANTE

DIMENSIONS

Min/max front legroom 900/1020mm **Min/max front headroom** 800/840mm
Min/max rear legroom 400/600mm **Interior width front/rear** 1550/1160mm
Min/max boot width 1090/1410mm **Boot height** 380mm **Boot volume** 178litres/dm³
Front/rear tracks 1524/1530mm **Kerb weight** 1808kg **Width with mirrors** 1990mm

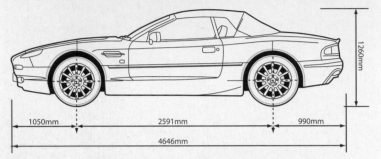

1260mm
1050mm 2591mm 990mm
4646mm

ENGINE

Layout	6 cyls in line, 3239cc
Max power	335bhp at 5750rpm
Max torque	361lb ft at 3000rpm
Specific output	103bhp per litre
Power to weight	185bhp per tonne
Torque to weight	200lb ft per tonne
Installation	Front, longitudinal, rear-wheel drive
Construction	Alloy head and block
Bore/stroke	91/83mm
Valve gear	4 per cyl, dohc
Compression ratio	8.3:1
Ignition and fuel	EDIS distributorless ignition, sequential fuel injection, Eaton supercharger, intercooler

CHASSIS AND BODY

Body	2dr convertible, Cd 0.31
Wheels	8Jx18in
Made of	Cast alloy
Tyres	245/40 ZR18 Bridgestone Expedia
Spare	Full size

TRANSMISSION

Gearbox	5-speed manual		
Ratios/mph per 1000rpm			
Final drive ratio	3.5:1		
1st	3.55/5.9	2nd	2.04/10.2
3rd	1.40/14.9	4th	1.00/20.9
5th	0.75/27.7		

STEERING

Type Rack and pinion, power assisted
Turns lock-to-lock 2.5
Turning circle 12.3m

SUSPENSION

Front Independent double wishbones, coil springs, anti-roll bar
Rear Independent double wishbones, coil springs

BRAKES

Front 284mm ventilated discs
Rear 305mm plain discs
Anti-lock Standard

Despite this, Aston Martin has not lost its sporting pedigree. The DB7's body control is exemplary, and rarely does the car feel all its 1808kg. To soften the car, Aston deleted the rear anti-roll bar; as a result it has lost a little sharpness of the coupé, especially on turn in. Nonetheless, it's a creditable effort.

Lean really hard on the ultra low profile Bridgestone Expedia 245/40 ZR18s, and a massive amount of predictable and reassuring grip looks after the Volante's driver. The chassis is incredibly secure, and it's only under extreme provocation that it can be encouraged to step out.

In a nutshell, this chassis is short on intimidation and big on ability. It's at its best at seven tenths, sprinting across wide open A roads. At times like this, few cars can match the uncomplicated joy that the Volante offers.

ECONOMY ★★★
Fuel economy acceptable, but inaccurate fuel gauge slashes the range

---

Although buying a Volante makes an extra £7450 dent in your bank balance over the coupé, it shouldn't add to your fuel bill. In most respects it betters the figures we recorded in the coupé, albeit by a negligible margin.

The one thing which still proves exceptionally irritating is the pessimistic fuel gauge warning light, which blinks on with about 30 litres of fuel still remaining in the generous 89-litre tank. At our touring route pace the range is an impressive 515 miles. But believe the little needle and you'll stop after only 350 miles.

This aside, it performs quite well considering its mass and power. A touring figure of 26.3mpg is perfectly respectable, meaning an owner could expect to top 20mpg during normal driving.

SAFETY AND EQUIPMENT ★★★★
Build and interior improved, but electric roof not as effective as the 500SL's

---

The hood on this car is absolutely magnificent in all but two respects. Its five layers cosset those inside when it's erected and wind noise is kept to a minimum. It also looks great when up. But, compared with a Mercedes SL, it is neither as easy to lower nor as attractive to look at when it's down.

The SL needs just the press of a button to lower

Cruise control buttons oddly located in centre console

Six speaker Alpine stereo system standard, but view is obstructed by gear lever in third and fifth

Graphics on instrument binnacle revised for ease of clarity

its roof; for the DB7, there are two clips to undo and a tonneau cover to clip on. When down, it stands quite high; as a result, rearward vision is somewhat obscured.

Elsewhere, both coupé and Volante DB7 cabins have undergone a minor revamp for 1996. The changes are relatively minor, but important in such an expensive car.

Having consulted 50 of the first 75 buyers, Aston set to work righting the wrongs. Once planted in the driver's seat, the first change you'll notice is a revised seat back. The old one had the driver sitting on rather than in the seat; it's better now. The electric seat controls have moved backwards as well, away from the driver's knees. Helping further to improve the driving position is a rake and reach adjustable steering wheel; previously it adjusted only for rake.

Aside from the driving position itself, the instrument graphics have been improved. It's safer too, with the addition of a passenger airbag at the expense of the glovebox. The Connolly hide

ABOVE Two-tone leather won't suit everybody, but Connolly trimmed cabin is much better built than early cars.

LEFT Token back seats.

Extra torque is paid for every time you fill up.

WHAT IT COSTS

ASTON MARTIN DB7 VOLANTE

On-the-road price	£89,950
Price as tested	£89,950
Cost per mile	na

INSURANCE

Insurance/typical quote   20/na

WARRANTY

12 months/unlimited mileage, 12 months anti corrosion, 12 months recovery, additional 12/24 months warranty £1290/£2679

SERVICING

Major 30,000 miles, 5 hours, £80 parts
Interim 7,500 miles, 3 hours, £60 parts

EQUIPMENT CHECKLIST

Automatic transmission	nco
Remote central locking	■
Electric windows front	■
Electric hood	■
Stereo/RDS/CD autochanger	■/■/■
Full Connolly leather	■
Air conditioning	■
Electric seats	■
Traction control	-
Airbag driver/passenger	■/■
Anti-lock brakes	■
Alarm/immobiliser	■/■
Trip computer/cruise control	-/■

■ = Standard   na = not available

still creaks from time to time, but this DB7 is much better built than the first cars. That said, it is still a very pricey alternative to a Mercedes 500SL, and an even pricier one to Jaguar's wonderful XK8 convertible.

MARKET & FINANCE ★★★
Still loses value too fast and build quality questionable; improving though

At £90,000, the Volante will be a rare sight on our roads, as only a mere handful of used examples will be concentrated at Aston dealers. Despite their very high image and prohibitive cost, the Astons are quite high depreciators in the class. Their cause has not been assisted by the introduction of Jaguar's XK8 at far less cost.

Buyers of new Volantes can expect to lose at least 20 per cent of their initial outlay within the first year, which compares badly with the likes of Ferrari

Two words best describe the DB7 Volante. Hugely desirable. The appeal of this Aston Martin grows as you spend more time in the car. After a few hundred miles, the finer points of Aston Martins' latest creation really begin to take hold. The small changes aren't revolutionary, but make a big difference to your view of the car as a whole. And it's great that, at long last, the handsome alloy wheels can be seen in their full glory. Previously, they had been hidden by giant Frisbee-style wheeltrims.

But if there is one single area where the Volante really scores, it's the ease with which an average driver can confidently enjoy the delights this car offers. For a machine of such mass and potential, it is extremely user friendly. Like its coupé counterpart, this Volante will one day become part of Aston's more precious heritage and it's set to become a car that Britain can be proud of now and in years to come.

It's not perfect; as always, the pace of development moves along at relentless speed, and in this case it's the XK8 convertible that is forcing the game along. Not only is it £35,000 cheaper than the Volante, it has a better engine and a superb automatic gearbox. Also this car fails at times to achieve the dizzy heights a £90,000 car should. In particular, the switchgear from mass production Fords and Mazdas is unwelcome, as is the less than perfect roof. And only die-hard enthusiasts would choose to change gear for themselves in this car. It needs more development. The automatic gearbox costs no extra and provides a more relaxed experience that most DB7 buyers will welcome.

Of the two, it is this DB7 which performs best, relatively speaking. At £89,950, you've really got to want this car. As overpriced as it seems, though, there's never been a better DB7 on sale.

Superbly engineered Volante is a winner   ★★★★

355 Spiders – they lose only nine per cent – and the cheaper Porsche 911 Carrera Cabrio, which loses 12 per cent in its first year.

Age and mileage is normally unkind to used Astons, and long-standing suspicions about reliability tend to accelerate the depreciation curve as they get older. DB7s will retain value better than any previous Aston – as the coupé has already proved – but now that new and used DB7 coupés are available in numbers, their residual values are falling away quite noticeably. It goes without saying that any used Volante will have to be in impeccable condition with a cast-iron history and a low mileage to attract buyers at this level; and older examples will eventually have stiff opposition from Mercedes SLs, the aforementioned Ferrari and Porsche models, and the similar looking XK8. Top priced cars will remain at Aston dealers, who will be able to charge prices over and above those of the rest of the used car market.

POWER BROKER

PROJECT VANTAGE Project Vantage is more than just a high-tech showcase. Its 6.0-litre V12, advanced construction and muscular styling give a clear glimpse of the next new Aston. *By Steve Cropley*

A brilliant new V12-engined Aston Martin Vantage concept car, which bristles with advanced technology and underlines the marque's determination to stay in the 200mph 'full house' GT car business beyond 2000, is proving to be a smash hit at this year's Detroit Motor Show.

The car, a fully detailed running prototype called Project Vantage, is styled by TWR's Ian Callum, who designed its highly successful four-year-old stablemate, the DB7. It is built by a partnership between Ford AVT (Advanced Vehicle Technology) and leading Ford suppliers, and is powered by a much-developed version of AVT's 6.0-litre V12, first seen in the Indigo show car two years ago. Finance also comes from Ford's advanced technology coffers, with the project intended to demonstrate how Aston Martin can become a showcase for its parent company's technology in future.

Built in around nine months, Project Vantage is the result of an idea shared by Aston Martin's chairman, Bob Dover, and Ford President Jac Nasser, who appointed him. It was Nasser who earmarked the "substantial" (but undisclosed) funds for the project. Nasser, who belongs to the Aston Martin Owners Club and owns a DB4, believes Aston Martin is "every bit as important and significant to Great Britain as Ferrari is to Italy." Both Nasser and Dover insist that Project Vantage will not be built as is, but will be used to gauge the reaction of dealers, customers and other critics as a guide to future products.

Despite all the management caution, the new Vantage's shape and specification answer many of the pressing questions that have surrounded Aston Martin since the launch of the DB7 sent production shooting up from 100 to 700 cars

a year, put another Aston Martin location – Bloxham, Oxfordshire – on the map, and showed that Aston Martin had a chance.

First, it shows that Aston has its eye on a two-tier model range – perhaps even a three-tier range if it ever builds Lagonda saloons as some of its management would like. Second, Project Vantage introduces a high-tech, low-tooling method of construction in aluminium honeycomb, carbon fibre and composite materials, specifically designed to allow hand-manufacture of cars at Newport Pagnell. Third, Project Vantage – and particularly its V12 engine – shows that Aston Martin's bosses see no need to stick to either the straight six or V8 engines that have become usual since the war.

Fourth, and perhaps most important, Project Vantage's under-body engineering is so thorough and complete (down to catalyst specification fuel tank location) that it's virtually certain to produce some new Aston, if not precisely this one. Bob Dover won't be drawn on the precise direction of the company's plans (see panel on page 27), but he sees total production rising from the present 600 cars a year to around 1000 in several years time. Despite Jac Nasser's Ferrari allusion, Newport Pagnell has no plans to match the Italian company's volume of 4000 cars a year, a rate Dover jokingly refers to as "the mass market."

Apart from the fact that the materials are completely different, Project Vantage's chassis bears an interesting similarity to the 37-year-old Jaguar. E-type. It has a unitary cabin section, with a tubular space frame attached to the firewall to carry the engine and front suspension.

There, however, the similarity stops. The Vantage's cabin section is made of aluminium

'WE RECKON ON SOMETHING OVER 450BHP, BUT REALLY, IT'LL PRODUCE PRETTY WELL WHATEVER WE NEED'

FEATURE

7 JANUARY 1998

Volume 215

No 1 I 5262

ABOVE From the moment you first clap eyes on it, Project Vantage satisfies the eye.

OPPOSITE Detail execution of concept amazing; striking alloys also a Callum effort; exact output of V12 not decided, but Aston suggests over 450bhp.

honeycomb sheet and carbon composite mouldings, framed by aluminium extrusions. The components are all adhesive-bonded into a self-jigging structure which is hugely stiff, yet also very light. The tubular front cradle is fabricated in aluminium, then bonded into the main monocoque.

The elegant out panels are non-stressed, and also made of aluminium. Dover says that Aston Martin has yet to decide whether – if it built a car like this – the panels would be hand-formed, as they are on today's V-cars, or part-formed by machine. Either way, the finishing would be done at Newport Pagnell, much as it always has.

The whole chassis, designed and tested on computer, is claimed to be twice as rigid as any previous big Aston. Even more impressive is the kerb weight: engineers are working to a target of 1500kg, 1000kg less than the present Vantage.

Small wonder, in the light of this, that Dover is rather casual about the eventual output of his car's quad-cam, 48-valve, all-alloy 6.0-litre V8. "We reckon on something over 450bhp," he says, "but really, it'll produce pretty well whatever we need." Engineers

estimate that the car will sprint to 60mph in just four seconds, reach the end of a standing quarter mile at 140mph, yet return better than 20mpg when cruising on a light throttle.

Since its appearance in the Indigo, the Ford AVT V12 has had much development at Cosworth, and can now meet and exceed the world's strictest exhaust emissions standards. Ford engineers make great play of the car's ability to accommodate a nine-litre catalyst; impending laws will soon require cars to have cats with a capacity one and a half times their engine size, they contend, and many fast car makers are having trouble accommodating such big canisters beneath their cars.

The Vantage's suspension is all independent, by double wishbones all round. The rear layout is relatively conventional, but the front suspension units are connected to the lower wishbones by pushrods, and laid longitudinally beside the engine to anchor into the firewall, the stiffest part of the car.

The layout is used for packaging reasons: the engine is big, and the designers wanted to keep the bonnet low. When fully developed, the car will use an electro-hydraulic active roll-control system developed by TWR, which positions rams at the ends of the car's anti-roll bars to counter sway as cornering forces build.

Steering is power-assisted rack and pinion, brakes are massive AP Racing units of 352mm diameter with six-pot callipers and standard anti-lock, and the car meets the road on massive Callum-designed 19x9in wheels with 255/40 ZR Bridgestones at the front and 285/40s behind.

From the moment you first clap eyes on it, Project Vantage satisfies the eye. It is a very big two-seater coupé, a little longer (though it doesn't look it) than the existing V8 coupé. Its spectacular, muscular shape is brought to life by finely resolved details which are typical of Ian Callum's design. The relationship with the more beautiful, more shapely DB7 is immediately obvious, though the two cars are quite different. The Vantage hugs the ground as if squeezed by its race-bred aerodynamics – suggested at the rear by its under-body venture.

Project Vantage is "a bit like a DB7 on steroids," says Callum, who is head of TWR Design at Leafield, Oxfordshire. It's a description which seems likely to stick. "The DB7 was deliberately built to be a beautiful car, a more sophisticated and restrained shape than the big Astons that were in production,"

ASTON BOSS HAS BIG DECISIONS AHEAD

"Don't tell people that we're going to build this car," says Aston boss Bob Dover from the other side of the boardroom table, fixing me and my notebook with a beady stare. "We may eventually build something like it, but we probably won't decide what to do until the end of this year."

Dover understands how excited people are inclined to get over cars like Project Vantage; how they might hype things rather too much. He was formerly chief programme engineer on the also-evocative Jaguar XK8, a job he carried out with distinction.

But despite the fact that he's a car guy to his back teeth, Dover simply doesn't want to talk future product. "The job," he says, "is to decide what sells, and then to make it. At the moment, we're still in the process of deciding."

"Will we build a DB8 or a DB9, or just re-create the V-car? I really don't know," says Dover. "Will we do a V12 or a V10? I don't know that either. To tell the truth, the V8 is still an option. We really haven't decided anything yet, and we intend to take most of 1998 to decide.

"But believe me, reaction to Project Vantage is going to be very important in what we decide. I'd say it was critical."

For all his reticence, Dover admits that time limits are starting to press Aston Martin. The present venerable V8 engine, which was new back at the beginning of the 1970s, will certainly not meet the emissions standards which are little more than two years away – whereas Project Vantage's V12 can meet them now.

Big changes are clearly on the horizon. But Dover vows that there will be no lash-up, no short-term solution to the pressing issues. Aston Martin has had too many of those. "We'll think a lot," he says. "Then we'll do it once, and get it right."

ABOVE Front grille reminiscent of DB4.

OPPOSITE Short overhangs, roof and rear side windows reminiscent of Zagato-designed Astons; superbly finished interior was designed by Neil Simpson, TWR colleague of Ian Callum; Project Vantage interior eschews traditional wood in favour of aluminium and carbon fibre.

he explains. "Having done that, I had to get more aggressive again with Project Vantage, to stress the car's extra potential without losing its Aston purity. We pulled its front wheels forward, gave the car a very high belt line – an important Aston characteristic – and moved the wheels as far out in the arches as we could, even closer than on the DB7. I wanted to give the feeling that it really belonged to the ground, that despite the performance it was anchored there no matter what."

Callum, who admires past Astons and particularly the DB4 GT Zagato, has unashamedly drawn on traditional Aston cues for Project Vantage. The short overhangs, and the shape of the roof and rear side window are reminiscent of Zagato-designed Astons; the grille (the last major styling issue to be decided) is reminiscent of the DB4.

Callum does not feel limited by these old Aston icons. In fact, he does not believe a new Aston should be too fashionable. "There has to be a

classical, traditional aspect to most luxury products," he explains, "because they last a long time in production. Project Vantage acknowledges trends, but it doesn't bow to them."

"We've set out to signal a very big change with the interior design," says Bob Dover. "There's no wood in it at all; we've used the aluminium and carbon, which actually make up so much of the car's structure. After all, wood only came into cars because that's what they were actually constructed of. We're also concentrating on the driver's true needs, so we've left out some luxury items like memory seats. Conversations with owners make us think they won't miss things like that."

The interior is the work of Neil Simpson, one of Ian Callum's TWR colleagues. Apart from the carbon and brushed aluminium, it features tan-coloured leather to cover its door inners, deep bucket seats, dominating fascia and high centre console, and even its four-point harnesses and headlining, which is

'THERE CAN BE NO DOUBT THAT A NEW, FULL-SIZE ASTON WILL COME OUT OF THIS PROJECT'

quilted much as it was in old Aston competition cars. There is a very prominent centre console, trimmed mainly with aluminium and carbon fibre, which runs into a high centre tunnel that carries on right down the centre of the cabin.

The fascia is like that of no production Aston. Ahead of the driver are four white-faced instruments (two big, two small) grouped under a hood, which is shaped to repeat the outline of the car's grille. Despite the generous use of hard, high-tech materials, there's no feeling of coldness or alienation, perhaps due to the warmth of the leather's rich tan.

Primary controls are on stalks below the awkward-looking airbag wheel, but the real eye-catchers are a pair of elegant aluminium gearchange paddles: this car mates a Borg-Warner six-speed gearbox with an electronic paddle-shift mechanism, designed by Magneti Marelli. It can give instant manual shifts or allow the driver to adopt automatic mode for more relaxing travel. The driver selects Drive of Reverse buttons via a panel mounted on the centre console. In the centre of that panel is a large red starter button, which lights when the ignition key is turned. The idea, says Simpson, is to give a heightened sense of occasion when the driver starts the engine.

This car is strictly a two-seater, with elegant leather-covered luggage bins behind the driver and passenger. But there is clearly room for a pair of occasional seats – or more space if the car were extended, which its ingenious construction is believed to allow. The boot isn't very long, but it is deep and easily wide enough to accommodate the two sets of golf clubs all US buyers seem to demand at this price level.

Both Ford and Aston Martin are extremely cagey about the future of Project Vantage, despite the fact that show cars rarely have the plausibility of shape, mechanical layout, construction and manufacturing details of this one. There can be no doubt that a new, full-size Aston will come out of this project, but its creators are absolutely determined not to be rushed. They won't decide, they say, until the back-end of the year – though how they'll react when the first Florida millionaire offers to buy the prototype is another thing.

Taking time to consider is not something cash-strapped managements at Newport Pagnell have previously had in their list of options. Old-time Aston-watchers will think it a nice change.

DB7 VANTAGE

Take the most successful Aston Martin ever. Add a 420bhp V12 engine. The result? 185mph and 0–60mph in 5.0sec. *By Steve Cropley*

Aston Martin's DB7, fast but never outrageously fast, will soon be joining the ranks of the true tyre-smokers. This week at the Geneva Motor Show the wraps come off a new, 420bhp V12-engined Vantage version. Delivers of both coupé and convertible will begin in the summer, close to the 40th anniversary of Aston's historic Le Mans victory in June 1959.

The Vantage's combination of 20 per cent more power, 17 per cent more torque, a new set of six close-ratio gears and only a few kilograms of extra weight pushes the manual car's top speed up from 160mph to a claimed 185mph, slices nearly a second from the 0–60mph time (Aston claims 5.0sec), and more than two seconds from the six-cylinder car's 0–100mph time of 14.4sec.

For this, and a well-equipped, luxuriously leathered cabin with redesigned instruments and seats, the buyer is expected to pay between £100,000 and £110,000, a premium of about £20,000 over the 335bhp six-cylinder car. Available at no extra cost will be a five-speed automatic version which is claimed to add a mere 0.1sec to the 0-60mph time.

Although Aston Martin intends to build the six-cylinder car while demand continues – another year seems likely – there is little doubt that the Vantage is the car that bosses want to catch the buyer's eye from now on. The straight six DB7 has done a fine job of restarting the DB model line, and providing Aston with a much-needed means of staying in business in the early '90s when the cupboard was otherwise bare.

But the V12's chief task is to answer the major criticism of the six: that it lacks a sense of occasion. Aston boss Bob Dover won't predict how demand will split between the six and 12 in the early months, but says they can be built side by side in whatever proportion the market demands. The V12's body is based closely on the original car's much-admired shape, styled by TWR Design's Ian Callum in the pre-Ford days when Tom Walkinshaw was an Aston director and TWR Engineering was charged with bringing the DB7 to production. Callum's main task has been to give the car a "tougher" look by making the sills more prominent, and increasing the size of the air intakes above and below the front bumper, which also provides more cooling for the bigger engine. He has also designed a new set of multi-spoke alloy wheels.

Although key areas like the roof, bonnet and door skins are unaltered, the car definitely looks more purposeful, and has visual links with Callum's project Vantage show car. The DB7's monocoque steel chassis, clad with panels that are both aluminium (main body) and composite (wings, bonnet, bootlid, bumpers), has needed relatively little modification, probably because the V12 is similar in length and weight to the supercharged six. DB7 project manager Dave King says that installing the V12 did give his people the opportunity to stiffen the structure along the transmission tunnel, improving torsional rigidity by around five per cent. This mainly benefits the Vantage Volante, which is said to resist scuttle shake unusually well for an open car.

Aston is keen to stress that the 5935cc alloy-block engine is all-new, and is used nowhere else in the Ford empire. Yet the V12's provenance is well known: it began life as an experimental engine formed from two Ford Duratec V6s and appeared for the first time in the Indigo show car a little over three years ago. In the intervening time it has been redesigned and prepared for production by Cosworth Technology. Its castings come from the same foundry as Ford's V10 grand prix engines.

QUICK FACTS

Model	Aston Martin DB7 Vantage
Price	£100,000 (est)
On sale	Summer 1999
0–60mph	5.0sec
Top speed	185mph

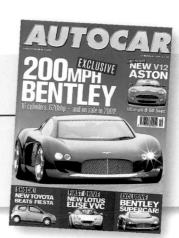

THE MAN BEHIND THE LINES

"When a decision was made to build the DB7 V12," says Ian Callum, designer of the world's most successful Aston Martin, "there was some discussion over whether we should change its shape at all. I was a bit unsure about changing it, because naturally enough I'd tried to make the original design as close to perfect as I could."

It must have been a lively debate. The original DB7 shape, drawn by TWR Design boss Callum in the early '90s, in the role of consultant to Aston Martin, is widely regarded as being not only the best-looking GT of the modern era, but also a brilliant expression of Aston marque values.

"I soon saw that the car had to change," Callum says, "once I'd realised it was going to be faster, more aggressive, more expensive and the air intakes had to be bigger because of the new engine. Once you understand a car's altered function, you can see what needs doing.

"We deepened the sides – visually, not actually – to make the whole thing look closer to the ground, and did the same with the nose. I was quite pleased that the grille had to be bigger because my one criticism of the original DB7 was that the grille was a bit small. The only way of doing it was to create the combination fog/indicator lights, which allowed me room to make the grille bigger. The inspiration for those came from the DBR1, the '50s Le Mans sports/racer, which had air intakes in just the same place. I'm pretty pleased with the way those worked out."

The V12's multi-spoke wheels were a particular challenge, says Callum. "I wanted them to reflect light best when viewed from three-quarter front or three-quarter rear. From dead side-on the spokes would be like blades, and you'd look straight through to those huge cross-drilled discs and Aston Martin-badged calipers. In sunshine, from the front, they look like a series of flickering blades."

Interestingly, Callum says he designed the DB7 V12 before Project Vantage – widely tipped as the basis for the next 'big' Aston – even though the two cars have been revealed to the public in reverse order. The bigger car – which could be given an engine with 590 or even 600bhp – takes the DB7 Vantage's aggressive look and adds its own more angular styling elements. Even so, the two cars are very definitely peas out of the same pod.

With twin chain-driven overhead camshafts, four valves per cylinder, oil-cooling of its pistons, a set of beautifully fabricated stainless steel exhaust headers and some of the most sophisticated engine management electronics around, King rates his new engine as one of the world's best and most modern V12s. It is relatively low stressed, too. Peak power of 420bhp is developed at 6000rpm, and the engine can be safely revved to 7000rpm. Maximum torque of 4000lb ft is developed fairly high in the rev range at 5000rpm, but King says his dyno tests show that 340lb ft is available not far above idle. "It will sing a song for you," says King, "or it will pull you around effortlessly at low revs. Either driving style is fine."

Aston's engineers have worked hard to produce the right engine note for the V12, while complying with draconian drive-by noise regulations. "The engine has a purposeful sound," says King, "and we think it's recognisable as a V12. We think the market is going to like it."

That's a diplomatic way of saying that the engineers have laboured to make the V12 sound more impressive than the rather uninspiring supercharged six.

The Vantage's six-speed manual gearbox is by Tremec (Borg Warner's new owner). Unlike the other cars that use the same 'box – Chrysler Viper, Chevrolet Corvette – it employs a special set of ratios without their ultra-tall top gearing. The Aston's

32mph per 1000rpm still provides relaxed cruising, but also reasonable acceleration in top. Automatic versions use the same ZF five-speeder as the BMW 7-series and Rolls-Royce Silver Seraph, with its electronic controls suitably modified for sporty responses.

Although the specification sheet shows no difference in the suspension fundamentals between DB7 and DB7 Vantage, the truth is that the V12's system has been extensively redesigned. The front's coil-sprung double wishbones have different dimensions to reduce the front wheels' scrub radius and accommodate the massive 355mm diameter ventilated and cross-drilled disc brakes. At the rear is a coil-sprung independent set-up with a huge lower link, and the half-shaft acting as the top link in traditional Jaguar style. Aston's engineers have also added a cross-shaped cage below the Vantage's diff to control axle tramp under full power and full braking, while doing very little to disturb ride refinement.

"The Vantage feels sharper and generally more

meaty in its responses," says King. "The V12's spring rates are 15 to 20 per cent stiffer than the six's, and there's more damping in both bump and rebound. We've sharpened the steering from 2.7 to 2.5 turns lock to lock, and we think this and

ABOVE Engineers went out of their way to give the 420bhp V12 an inspiring sound.

OPPOSITE Combined foglights/indicators inspired by intakes on '50s DBR1.

BELOW V12 is crucial to Aston's plans; bosses hope it will take the bulk of DB7 sales.

our suspension changes give the car the precise, purposeful feel it needs in its role as a GT with supercar performance,"

Not all of this talk of extra performance and sharpness applies to the Vantage Volante, which gets the new engine and engineering, but has slightly softer suspension rates because Aston's market experience shows that convertible buyers prefer it that way. Likewise, the Volante's top speed is limited to 165mph, possibly because fabric tops and three-mile-a-minute winds aren't really compatible.

Both V12 models use 245/40 ZR18 tyres on eight-inch rims at the front as before, but the offsets are different from those on the six-cylinder car's wheels to accommodate the bigger brakes. The rear tyres, which on the standard DB7 are the same size as the fronts, are 265/35 ZR18s on nine-inch rims. Aston admires the grip and lasting qualities of the Bridgestone SO2 tyre, and was fitting them to most of the DB7s we saw on a recent visit to the Bloxham factory.

The Ford culture is gradually permeating Aston, with growing benefit for the customer. Part of the two-year development programme for this new car has included subjecting it to Ford's tough PASCAR

ABOVE Luxurious leather-trimmed cabin features redesigned instruments and seats. Vantage is offered with six-speed manual gearbox or five-speed automatic.

durability tests, the same standards that the Jaguar S-type has been required to meet. The car has completed more than 100,000 miles of testing in extremes of heat and cold, and has generally had a tougher shakedown than any previous Aston.

The DB7 is already the most successful Aston in history, with more than 2000 cars sold since 1994. The Vantage is aiming at a total of 31 markets (dominated by a big four of the UK, Germany, the US and Japan) which is more than the hugely expensive, hand-built V8 model can reach. Dover has designs on producing 1000 cars a year, which is 300–500 more than he's making now. He is reticent about his plans, but his task seems to be to keep DB7 production at capacity (600 a year) with the V12, while he replaces the V8 models in a year or so, probably with a development of Project Vantage. Then he'll move on to the DB7's replacement – already believed to be well advanced on Callum's drawing board – in 2002 or 2003.

If that is truly the shape of things to come, the DB7 Vantage's role looks utterly crucial. Far from being a mere add-on model, it is the car which maintains the ground gained by the original DB7, while the company gets on with the rest of its life.

BELOW Larger sills make Vantage appear closer to ground. Huge brake discs visible through bespoke 18in alloys.

SPECIFICATIONS DB7 VANTAGE

ECONOMY

Combined mpg na

DIMENSIONS

Length	4666mm
Width	1830mm
Height	1238mm
Wheelbase	2591mm
Weight	1780kg
Fuel tank	89 litres

ENGINE

Layout	12 cyls in a vee, 5935cc
Max power	420bhp at 6000rpm
Max torque	400lb ft at 5000rpm
Specific output	71bhp per litre
Power to weight	236bhp per tonne
Installation	Longitudinal, front, rwd
Bore/stroke	89/79.5mm
Made of	Alloy heads and block
Compression ratio	10.3:1
Valve gear	4 per cyl, dohc
Ignition and fuel	Sequential electronic fuel injection

STEERING

Type Rack and pinion, power assisted
Turns lock-to-lock 2.5

GEARBOX

Type 6-speed manual
Ratios/mph per 1000rpm
Final drive ratio 3.77:1

1st 2.66/7.5		2nd 1.78/11.2	
3rd 1.30/15.3		4th 1.00/19.9	
5th 0.80/25.0		6th 0.63/31.7	

SUSPENSION

Front Double wishbones, coil springs and dampers, anti-roll bar
Rear Independent double wishbones, coil springs and dampers, anti-roll bar

BRAKES

Front 355mm ventilated discs
Rear 330mm discs

WHEELS AND TYRES

Size 8Jx18in (f), 9Jx18in (r)
Made of Alloy
Tyres 245/40 ZR18 (f), 265/35 ZR18 (r)

THE **AUTOCAR** VERDICT

Supercar performance combined with a more muscular interpretation of the DB7's gorgeous lines. We can't wait to drive it.

All figures are manufacturer's claims

DB7 VANTAGE

When the Aston Martin DB7 arrived in 1994 it heralded the future for the great British marque. Only the unrealistic could possibly be opposed to Ford's ownership of Aston

The new DB7 Vantage is further proof of this. Not only does it have an all-new Cosworth-developed V12 engine that produces 420bhp, but substantial changes have also been made to the chassis.

The six-cylinder DB7 is an unquestionably beautiful car. Beautiful, but not without flaws under the skin. In performance and refinement it falls behind its rivals. The Vantage promises to right these wrongs, while reaffirming Ford's commitment to making future Aston Martins worthy of the badge.

DESIGN AND ENGINEERING ★★★★
Much more thorough job than just fitting a V12

The Aston Martin Db7 is in *Autocar*'s opinion one of the world's most beautiful cars, and there is little doubt that it will take a place in history as such. It is hard to find anything about the shape to criticise.

Even so, Aston has made slight changes to the DB7 that wears the famous Vantage name. The sills are more pronounced, the grille is now filled with horizontal bars, and the driving lamps and indicators have been combined. The changes are subtle but ably distinguish the Vantage from the six-cylinder model that will continue alongside it.

There are a host of changes under the svelte skin, but we will come to those after we have looked

QUICK FACTS

Model	DB7 Vantage
Price	£92,500
Top speed	185mph
30–70mph	4.2sec
0–60mph	5.2sec
60–0mph	3.2sec
For	Spread of power, fabulous engine note,
Against	Lifeless steering, cramped interior

at the engine. Essentially it is a mating of two Ford
Duratec V6 engines as fitted to the Mondeo and
Cougar, but there's far more to it than that.

Cosworth is responsible for engine manufacture,
from casting to assembly and testing. Similar to
the TWR-built six, a plaque on top of the engine
identifies the inspector who signed off the car before
it left Aston's Bloxham factory.

This 6.0-litre V12 is a wonderful motor, and
looks good to boot. Looks very good on paper, too.
Take 420bhp at 6000rpm and 400lb ft of torque at
5000rpm, for starters. The torque is spread evenly
right through the lower end of the rev range. Part of
the design brief was to build an engine that was very
tractable low down, but produced strong power all
the way to the red line.

No corners have been cut with the Vantage. The
manual car that we have tested here (a five-speed
automatic gearbox, as used in the BMW 750i, is also
available) is fitted with the Tremec six-speed gearbox
that's also used in the Corvette and Viper. The
difference is that Aston has fitted the transmission
with closer ratios that match the engine perfectly.

And so to the changes under the skin. The area
around the bulkhead and transmission tunnel has

been made much stiffer in order to improve torsional
rigidity. The redesign should really show its benefit in
the soft-top Volante.

The upper and lower front wishbones are new,
as is a vertical link. At the rear an additional link has
been fitted to cope with the extra torque. To finish
off, stiffer springs front and rear are wrapped around
new gas-filled Bilstein dampers.

PERFORMANCE AND BRAKES ★★★★
The Vantage goes hard and stops harder

The DB7 is a completely different car in Vantage
form. The supercharged six that lives in the standard
car is an interesting engine, but somewhat agricultural.
Its 335bhp is delivered to an accompaniment of
wheezes and whirs from the blown motor that
sometimes sounds a little too mechanical for its own
good. The six does a fair enough job, but it feels
ancient and a 0–60mph time of 5.8sec is no more
than average, especially for a car with an Aston Martin
badge on its nose. The new V12 changes all that.

As is the current vogue, a red starter button
mounted on the centre of the console fires up the
motor. The engine starts and runs smoothly and

sounds great to boot, even at idle. Only Lamborghini builds a V12 that sounds better.

Cutting a new set of ratios for the gearbox could not have been cheap, but it is money well spent. The Vantage feels even quicker than the 0-60mph time of 5.2sec suggests. The car launches hard in first gear and pulls hard through the next three gears.

Although the V12 sounds happy (and wonderful) right up to its 7000rpm rev limit, you'll only need to use about 5000rpm for extremely rapid progress. This ability to pull hard in the mid-range enables the Vantage to polish off slower cars with confidence-inspiring ease.

The gearshift is not quick and the throws are long, but the improvement over the original DB7 in both performance and feel is dramatic. Extracting maximum performance from the six-cylinder engine is rather a chore and shows up the car's weaknesses. The harder you try to drive it, the less rewarding the experience. In truth, the six-cylinder car is at its best on continental motorways, where it will cruise happily well into three figures.

The Vantage is a complete contrast. It, too, is a consummate grand tourer, but the difference is that the Vantage is a pleasurable car to drive quickly

ROAD TEST DB7 VANTAGE

MAXIMUM SPEEDS

6th	185mph/7000rpm	5th	175/7000
4th	139/7000	3rd	107/7000
2nd	78/7000	1st	53/7000

ACCELERATION FROM REST

True mph	seconds	speedo mph
30	2.3	32
40	3.0	42
50	4.1	53
60	5.2	63
70	6.5	73
80	6.5	84
90	9.8	94
100	11.8	105

Standing qtr mile 13.6sec/107mph
Standing km 25.3sec/140mph
30-70mph through gears 4.2sec

ACCELERATION IN GEAR

MPH	5th	4th	3rd	2nd
10–30	-	-	-	2.6
20–40	5.7	4.2	3.2	2.5
30–50	5.3	4.0	3.2	2.3
40–60	5.3	3.9	3.1	2.3
50–70	5.4	4.0	3.0	2.4
60–80	5.5	4.1	3.1	-
70–90	5.6	3.2	3.2	-
80–100	5.7	3.5	3.5	-

FUEL CONSUMPTION

Average/best/worst/touring
16.4/21.4/6.6/21.4mpg

Urban	9.7mpg
Extra urban	22.3mpg
Combined	15.1mpg
Tank capacity	88 litres
Touring range	420 miles

BRAKES

30/50/70mph	9.4/26.6/51.5 metres
60-0mph	3.2sec

NOISE

Idle/max revs in 3rd 52/83dbA
30/50/70mph 65/67/72dbA

TESTER'S NOTES

■ We reckon that an automatic Vantage Volante in British racing green with tan leather would be the car for Cannes in the summer.

■ The Vantage posted 6.6mpg fuel consumption during performance testing. We can't remember a car that drank more heavily.

■ Good grief, what do you get in an optional £295 first aid kit, as available on new Astons? Vouchers for a top doctor perhaps?

SPECIFICATIONS DB7 VANTAGE

DIMENSIONS

Min/max front legroom 910/1100mm Min/max front headroom 850/900mm
Min/max rear legroom 410/600mm Interior width front/rear 1450/1320mm
Boot volume 170/litres/dm³ Front/rear tracks 1524/1530mm Kerb weight 1622kg
Weight distribution front/rear 56/44 Width with/without mirrors 2036/1830mm

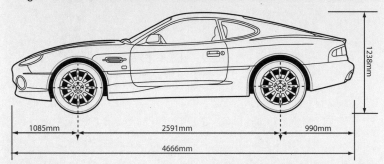

1085mm 2591mm 990mm
4666mm
1238mm

ENGINE

Layout	12 cyls in vee, 5935cc
Max power	420bhp at 6000rpm
Max torque	400lb ft at 5000rpm
Specific output	71bhp per litre
Power to weight	236bhp per tonne
Torque to weight	225lb ft per tonne
Installation	Longitudinal, front, rear-wheel drive

Construction	Alloy heads & block
Bore/stroke	89mm/79.5mm
Valve gear	4 per cyl, dohc
Compression ratio	10.3:1
Ignition and fuel	Electronic ignition, sequential fuel injection

CHASSIS AND BODY

Body	2dr coupé
Wheels	8Jx18in (f), 9Jx18in (r)
Made of	Cast alloy
Tyres	245/40 ZR18 (f), 265/35 ZR18 (r)
Spare	Space saver

TRANSMISSION

Gearbox	6-speed manual by Tremec		
Ratios/mph per 1000rpm			
Final drive	3.77		
1st	2.66/7.5	2nd	1.78/11.2
3rd	1.30/15.3	4th	1.00/19.9
5th	0.80/25.0	6th	0.63/31.7

STEERING

Type Rack and pinion, power assisted
Turns lock-to-lock 2.7
Turning circle 12.3m

SUSPENSION

Front Double wishbones, coil springs/damper, anti-roll bar
Rear Double wishbones, coil springs/dampers, anti-roll bar

BRAKES

Front 355mm ventilated discs
Rear 330mm ventilated discs
Anti-lock Standard

---

anywhere. The smoothness of the V12 and the thrust that's always available make it a joy to use the power to the full. Experience of the automatic gearbox in the BMW 750i leads us to expect that the automatic Vantage will be even more pleasant to use.

The Vantage is a very well rounded performer. This includes considerable stopping power. Large four-pot calipers at the front grip 355mm ventilated discs, and these brakes are quite breathtaking. As in the Porsche 911, you can brake later than you'd believe possible, and keep on doing it. What's more, the feel through the pedal is reminiscent of the 911, too. This is the braking set-up that the DB7's cousin, the Jaguar XKR, should have been fitted with.

HANDLING AND RIDE ★★★
Vague steering spoils the composed ride

By now you'll have realised that the thread running through this test is that Aston Martin has done more to the DB7 to create the Vantage than just dump in a larger and more powerful engine.

The standard DB7 works brilliantly as a sleek and beautiful grand tourer; few cars will bring you to your destination in greater style. But as we have already said in the performance section, once you start driving it like a sports car, its weaknesses start to show. The same goes for the car's dynamic abilities.

Judging by the depth of the work that Aston has carried out on the DB7's superstructure and suspension components for the V12 model, the company also felt that a lot needed to be done to put the Vantage's handling on a par with its performance.

Although the Vantage is fitted with higher rate springs than the DB7, the car rides even more smoothly than the six-cylinder car. The stiffening work done around the transmission tunnel and the revised wishbones and links have imbued the Vantage with excellent straight-line stability. That the suspension has a suppleness that absorbs bumps and scars in the road is also a major contributor to the predictable, secure feel at speed. The supple ride and stability blend well with the engine's effortless power.

Slip out of grand touring mode and into the sports car mindset and the flaws in the Aston's chassis start to make themselves known. The car's biggest weakness is its steering. The same can be said of the standard DB7, though thanks to the removal of several feel-robbing bushings in the steering column and linkages, the Vantage's steering is a definite improvement.

The actual steering weight can't be faulted. And the car is fitted with a quite wonderful wheel, wrapped in equally lovely leather. Amazing the difference a great steering wheel makes. You lightly grip the wheel and let the Vantage flow down the road. But push hard through corners and the steering feels slow and unresponsive. It's the one area on the car that needs serious attention.

Traction control and 265/35 rear tyres ensure that despite the torque available, the Vantage remains well behaved. Switch off the traction control, however, and the Aston's rear end can easily be made to slide. It's a particularly pleasant experience, as the rear tends to slide gently then suddenly gather momentum.

As a grand tourer the Vantage works well. Improve the steering and it will come alive elsewhere.

WHAT IT COSTS

ASTON MARTIN DB7 VANTAGE

On-the-road price	£92,500
Price as tested	£96,920
Cost per mile	na

INSURANCE

Insurance/typical quote	20/na

WARRANTY

24 months/unlimited mileage

SERVICING

Every 7500 miles or 6 months.

EQUIPMENT CHECKLIST

Satellite navigation	-
Anti-lock brakes	■
Airbag driver/passenger/side	■/■/-
RDS stereo/CD player	■/■
Alarm/immobiliser	■/■
Central locking/remote	■/■
Air conditioning	■
Leather upholstery	■
Traction control	■

■ = Standard na = not available

SAFETY AND EQUIPMENT ★★★★
Strictly a two-seater, ambience is wonderful

The DB7's interior is just what you'd hope to step into once you've taken in the car's beautiful exterior. The cabin is a demonstration of how to create a cosseting and characterful environment for seriously fast long-distance driving. Acres of luscious Connolly leather sweep around the interior, trimmed to a very high standard. It's just down to the customer to use good taste in selecting the colours.

Just as it is to select the exterior colour. Aston Martin will paint the car any colour, as long as the paint has a code number, at no extra cost.

You will still recognise large numbers of Ford-sourced switches dotted on the Aston's dashboard.

BELOW New DB7 Vantage points to a strong and secure future for Aston Martin.

ABOVE Vantage has subtle body changes such as more pronounced sills. More serious changes lie under the skin.

BELOW Boot space adequate for grand touring.

The difference is that many are from more modern Fords than those fitted to the first DB7s. There's little point in carping on about their suitability for an Aston Martin because their use is an economic reality. That said, there's no reason why a couple of machined alloy knobs couldn't replace the cheap Ford pieces used on the heater controls.

It's tempting to suggest that Aston does away with the DB7's rear seats altogether, as they are all but useless for seating anybody over six years old for anything more than a trip around the corner. An optional fire extinguisher mounted under the front of the seat squab made that seat useless for anyone with legs that reached floor level.

Up front, however, there are no complaints. The seats are comfortable, though they could provide rather more support. Our Vantage test car was fitted with a list of optional extras that included the expensive but excellent £595 sports steering wheel, the obtrusive £195 fire extinguisher, a £295 first aid kit, an umbrella holder in the boot for £195, audio upgrade at £1850, £995 oak veneer, and a heated front screen for £295. That adds up to £4420, which brings the total price for the car up to £96,920.

Even with these extras fitted, the Vantage is something of a bargain compared with the £84,950 six-cylinder DB7 and rivals such as the £149,701 Ferrari 550 Maranello.

ECONOMY ★★★
Slightly thirstier than the standard DB7

We can't remember a car that drank so heavily at the test track. The Vantage managed a very thirsty 6.6mpg. Fortunately, things improved considerably out on the road.

Over our touring route the 6.0-litre V12 returned 21.4mpg, which is much more sensible. By comparison, in our 1994 road test the six-cylinder car managed 26.2mpg over the same route. The numbers get closer when you average out the consumption figures. The six managed 17.1mpg overall and the Vantage 16.4. That gives a range of 320 miles from the 88-litre fuel tank.

MARKET & FINANCE ★★★★
Small build and market good for residuals

Despite the fact that the new DB7 Vantage will join the six-cylinder car in the range rather than replace it – Aston Martin dealers apparently reckon that there'll still be a market for the six – we'd be surprised if demand for the V12 wasn't substantial. It is, after all, only £8000 more than the six-cylinder car and a hugely more competent car to boot.

Residual values of DB7s are strong – even for early examples that didn't have a brilliant reputation for build quality. With only 600 cars being produced annually for an international market, demand is always strong. The even more desirable DB7 Vantage should be even more sought-after in the second-hand market.

AUTOCAR VERDICT

Without question the DB7 has put Aston Martin firmly back on the map. No other car in the company's history has been built in such large numbers. Now over 600 cars a year roll out of Aston's Bloxham factory. This success is not surprising – one look at the car explains it. The DB7's beautiful shape not only silences critics who say that it's a Jag in drag; it also allows many of the car's faults to be put to the back of the mind.

It was obvious that a Vantage version of the DB7 would eventually appear. What wasn't anticipated was just how special and how thorough a job would be done by Aston Martin – and, of course, by Ford, which has said that it intends Aston to be a showcase for its cutting edge technology. The Vantage certainly bears this out.

Few cars in history have benefited so greatly from the installation of a new engine. The supercharged six-cylinder engine sounded an extremely apt powerplant for a new Aston Martin, but in reality fell somewhat short. The birth of the Jaguar XKR made this even more apparent.

Aston Martin could have merely dropped the new V12 into the DB7 and produced the required performance. It could have done, but has instead chosen to do a much more comprehensive job. The Vantage outguns and outbreaks its junior sibling and is more comfortable and refined into the bargain.

The DB7 Vantage is a landmark model in the company's history. It is one of the best cars Aston has ever produced and it shows that there is a bright future for the company. Three weeks ago we pitched the Vantage against Ferrari's incredible 550 Maranello. The Aston came second, but by no great margin. There's a big margin in price, however: about £50,000.

Although the six-cylinder DB7 remains in production, we can see no reason to save £8000 and buy it instead of the Vantage. Sure, £92,500 is not cheap, but look back through your brown and curled copies of *Autocar* at old tests featuring Astons and you'll see that the Vantage is something of a bargain. Thanks to Ford's PASCAR test programme, the Vantage is likely to be the most reliable Aston in history, too. The Vantage is a big step towards putting Aston Martin on the road to greatness.

Double the cylinders, twice the car ★★★★

ASTON VANTASTIC

VANQUISH V12 Aston Martin's all-new super-coupé flagship is finally unveiled – and it's set to take the world by storm. *By Steve Cropley*

Step forward, Aston Martin Vanquish V12. At last, the Newport Pagnell firm's replacement for the 31-year-old V8 range is revealed – in photographs, if not in the flesh.

The new, £180,000 super-coupé won't be at the British Motor Show this year, partly because Aston's small team still has key improvements to add to the cars photographed here, and partly because 30 per cent of this year's production is already sold to advance customers in the US, so it hardly needs orders from the NEC show.

It was pretty clear, when Aston Martin showed its Project Vantage concept car around the motor shows a couple of years ago – and discussed, at length, an advanced aluminium-carbon composite construction process it had devised specifically for low-volume production – that this would be the basis for the new big Aston, nowadays codenamed AMV03.

The wonder is how close the car comes to Ian Callum's original design. According to Vanquish chief programme engineer Ian Minards, the main styling change is to the front and rear light clusters, which now have "custom designs" whereas Project Vantage's lights came from a convenient parts bin. "Of course, every panel is different in detail, as always happens when a car goes into production, but the key elements are all there," he says.

Thus the Vanquish keeps its strong styling links with the DB7, although it looks more muscular because of its bluff front and bigger grille, waisted body and mighty haunches. It also has clear links with

Astons of DB4–DB6 vintage, though its proportions and stance make it quite clearly an Aston of the third millennium. Callum, who remains Aston's director of design while holding down a similar position at Jaguar, believes the combination of DB7 and Vanquish has established the DNA of the modern Aston, from which future models can build.

It's clear that Vanquish customers will be people who appreciate its rarity (only about 300 will be built annually, at £170,000 to £200,000 a throw), its advanced construction and the bespoke nature of its equipment, paint and trim. In pure value terms, the Vanquish seems some way behind the latest, V12-engined DB7 Vantage, since it is tipped to weigh much the same at the kerb (1820kg), uses a developed version of the same engine (with 450bhp against 420) and is barely an inch longer overall.

The one Vanquish dimension markedly different from those of the DB7 is its four-inch-longer wheelbase (2690mm) which gives it a noticeably shorter front overhang and a stronger, tougher look. The extra wheelbase must also help with rear seat room, terribly restricted in the DB7. The Vanquish is available either as a two-seater or two-plus-two, an astute move by Aston, which knows well that most makers of fast coupés get regular orders for both layouts but usually choose to build only one of them.

Of course, the Vanquish's biggest claim to fame is likely to be performance. Aston Martin hasn't signed off the car's precise acceleration figures yet, but it promises a 0–60mph sprint time of around 4.7sec and a 0–100mph time under 10sec. The promised top-speed – 190mph – depends heavily, even in a car of the Vanquish's power, on a fairly low-drag body.

According to Minards, the drag factor will be 0.364, far better than most Astons of the past, but hampered a little by the car's bluff front and "tough" styling features.

There are no comments from Aston Martin HQ yet about a supercharged Vanquish Vantage version, but customers are sure to demand it and Aston has

QUICK FACTS

Model	Aston Martin Vanquish V12
Price	£180,000 (est)
On sale	Spring 2001
0–60mph	4.7sec (est)
Top speed	190mph (est)

FEATURE

11 OCTOBER 2000

Volume 226

No 2 | 5404

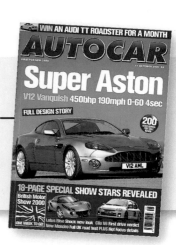

been willing in the past to build engines with outputs of up to 600bhp. Might we see a Vanquish which could pull 0–60mph in the late three-second bracket?

Beneath the skin the Vanquish is entirely different from its cheaper, older relative. Whereas the DB7 has a steel monocoque chassis, clothed in aluminium outer panels and intended for production levels of dozens a week (annual production at its Bloxham factory will rise to 1200 next year, double the original DB7 target of 1993), the Vanquish is a genuinely hand-finished automobile, built at Newport Pagnell in the tradition of the best-loved post-war Astons.

Its basic platform is an extruded aluminium structure, similar to but much larger than the Lotus Elise's chassis, bonded to which are carbon fibre parts in high-load areas like the door frames, transmission tunnel and screen pillars. The chassis is then built up with other composite components whose fibres are laid up using a new, more accurate robotic system for strength and repeatability. The whole lot is then bonded into a safety cell which far outstrips any previous Aston for bending or torsional rigidity (and meets all current safety standards). The process had its roots inside Tom Walkinshaw's TWR Groups several years ago, and was developed by structures expert Dan Parry-Williams, who at the time was working there with Callum.

The basic Vanquish shell arrives at Aston from Hydro Automotive Systems in Worcester – also the source for Lotus's core chassis parts – and is built up at the Newport Pagnell factory. The core chassis is clothed in aluminium panels in the traditional Aston Way, with a dozen Buckinghamshire artisans fitting each panel individually to the car.

What's different is the source of the panels. Many are Superformed, though some are still stamped in the old way. Aston Martin's aim, according to new chief executive Ulrich Bez, is to preserve its hand-manufacturing heritage, while using a modern process which can produce the strength and repeatability modern cars demand.

A by-product should be durability: older Astons have been ravaged by corrosion in the past, but the new variety should be all but impervious to it. To match this new-age durability, Aston engineers are claiming to have subjected the Vanquish to the most comprehensive and exhaustive test programme ever, amassing a million miles on 50 prototypes all over the world. There are some lurid ice-driving shots on a Vanquish promotional video that display the chassis balance well.

As a back-up, the car's components and systems have been tested on Ford R&D centre rigs around the world. It's clear that having adopted an entirely new construction system for its flagship, Aston is anxious that it should work.

The engine, the latest version of the 48-valve, 6.0-litre, 60-degree Duratec V12, is mounted north–south in the nose, driving the rear wheels. Now its power output is 450bhp at 6500rpm, and 410lb ft of torque at 5000rpm (though the curve is pretty flat, engineers say, from 2000rpm onwards). The engine uses a new management system from Visteon (Ford's

ABOVE New construction process uses carbon fibre composites and aluminium panels to improve strength and durability.

semi-detached components company) which is part of the central processor that also controls the transmission and the anti-theft system and is capable of up to two million commands a second.

In its latest version the engine has lightened valvetrain parts and a strengthened crankshaft There's a new air induction system, a drive-by-wire throttle, the camshafts are redesigned and the all-new stainless steel exhaust incorporates close-coupled catalysts which achieve full efficiency inside 30 seconds and reinforce the big V12's reputation for low emissions. The exhaust is clad over its entire length in aerospace-developed heat shielding, presumably because exhaust heat and composite structures make very poor bedfellows.

The Vanquish's transmission has its roots in the Borg Warner six-speed manual 'box used in the DB7 and many other high-torque cars, but its maker is now called Tremec, and it has a new paddle-shift

system from Magneti Marelli, which give the driver either full control of the shifting or recourse to an automatic mode which operates the gears without driver input. There is also a Winter mode which helps the driver avoid applying too much torque on low-grip surfaces, and a Sport mode which cuts shift times to a mere 300 milliseconds, at some cost to smoothness. Aston has high hopes for the system, which is standard. Want a stick shift? They'll build it for you especially, but it'll cost extra.

The engine and gearbox are carried just ahead of the driver and front passenger on a steel, aluminium

ABOVE Production car retains much of concept's original styling, although details like rear lights have been redesigned. High-quality construction due to hand-finishing process at Aston's Newport Pagnell headquaters.

BELOW Vanquish has clear links with DB7 and echoes '50s and '60s Astons like DB6.

and carbon fibre subframe which bolts directly into the front bulkhead. Aston Martin designers subscribe to the theory (rapidly being embraced at Ferrari, too) that front-engined cars should have something close to 50:50 weight distribution, to aid traction and keep the car's polar moments low. The longer wheelbase and smaller front overhang undoubtedly help here.

The suspension is an all-new system of forged alloy double wishbones and cast aluminium uprights, front and rear, with a coil spring and monotube damper for each wheel and an anti-roll bar at each end. The rear wheels receive drive from a limited-slip differential, which works in tandem with an electronic traction control to reduce engine power when it senses slippage and apply one or other rear brake in severe cases.

The tyres are 19-inch ZR-rated Yokohamas: 255/40 at the front and 285/40 behind, on multi-spoke alloy wheels which are similar to but a bit chunkier than those on the DB7 Vantage, which has 18-inch hoops with smaller sections.

Aston Martin intends to make specifying and buying a Vanquish a more enjoyable experience for its customers than ever before. Every buyer will be invited to the factory to choose specification, carpets, leather or Alcantara and trim colours. Minards says there's a "limitless" range of colours: each body gets eight coats of paint, is clad in eight Connolly hides and requires 12 square metres of Wilton carpet before it is completely trimmed.

Equipment will be far more comprehensive than past Astons, too. As well as their choice of two-seater or two-plus-two cabin layouts, customers will get a standard tyre pressure sensing system, rain-sensing wiper operation, an automatic twilight-sensing operation for the headlights, plus satellite navigation. Naturally, there will be a climate controlled cabin, and the hi-fi system will be among the best available.

Aston Martin' management is aware of being granted a degree of indulgence by its buyers – because of its low volume and its constant struggle against unprofitability – but neither Aston nor its masters in Dearborn believe they can continue to trade on people feeling sorry for it. New boss Bez, formerly of BMW and Porsche, feels particularly strongly that this is not a good foundation for a car maker aiming to be in the same arena as Ferrari and Ford.

One area receiving rapid development is cabin

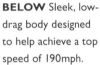

BELOW Sleek, low-drag body designed to help achieve a top speed of 190mph.

design. When the car was shown to journalists at Newport Pagnell recently, we weren't allowed to photograph the cabin. But the more corpulent hacks, who had complained about a lack of interior space, were assured by company officials that all would be well by the time the car reached production. Bez and Co are at present working on ways of lowering the driver's seat and finding more cabin space, and we're promised it will be changed in time for delivery of the first customer's car in the third quarter of 2001. Bez is content to be judged by this car by the time it reaches production.

Meanwhile, the new Aston Martin Vanquish has far more significance to the 78-year-old company that built it than merely as a new shape in the showroom. It replaces the whole "flagship" V8 line which began in 1969, and it introduces a manufacturing process which, while keeping the traditions of hand manufacture, brings a new flexibility to Newport Pagnell's operations which will allow it to vary versions and shapes more easily in future. We can expect to see far more exotic Aston (and Lagonda) offshoots, revealed more frequently, which is something we should all look forward to.

SPECIFICATIONS VANQUISH V12

ECONOMY

Combined mpg	na

DIMENSIONS

Length	4665mm
Width	1923mm
Height	1318mm
Wheelbase	2690mm
Weight	1820kg
Fuel tank	80 litres

ENGINE

Layout	12 cyls in vee, 5935cc
Max power	450bhp at 6500rpm
Max torque	410lb ft at 5000rpm
Specific output	76bhp per litre
Power to weight	247bhp per tonne
Installation	Front, longitudinal, rwd
Bore/stroke	89/79.5mm
Made of	Alloy heads & block
Compression ratio	10.5:1
Valve gear	4 per cyl, dohc per bank
Ignition and fuel	Visteon twin PTEC

engine management controlling ignition and fuel injection

SUSPENSION

Front and rear Double wishbones, coil springs, dampers, anti-roll bar

GEARBOX

Type 6-speed manual with auto mode
Ratios/mph per 1000rpm
Final drive ratio 3.69

1st 2.66/8.2	2nd 1.78/12.3
3rd 1.30/16.8	4th 1.00/21.9
5th 0.79/27.3	6th 0.63/34.9

STEERING

Type Rack and pinion, variable power assistance
Turns lock-to-lock 2.73 turns

BRAKES

Front 355mm cross-drilled ventilated discs
Rear 330mm ventilated discs

WHEELS AND TYRES

Size 9Jx19in (front), 10Jx19in (rear)
Made of Alloy
Tyres 255/40 ZR19 (front), 285/40 ZR19 (rear) Yokohama AML

THE **AUTOCAR** VERDICT

Powerful, attractive V12 flagship looks set to pave the way for an exciting and more successful future for the British marque.

All figures are manufacturer's claims

BEEF EXPORT

The rain is falling with tropical intensity. Droplets the size of shell cartridges shower on my head like pebbles. So I run for the Atlanta Hilton's protective canopy where, unexpectedly, I get my first look.

The Vanquish is an hour early for our rendezvous. It sits alone, unguarded, dripping wet, a barely perceptible curl of steam rising from a bonnet vent.

It's a hell of a moment. Ian Callum, the man responsible for the Vanquish's body language, has done a great thing because there's not a single angle on this car that doesn't look pure Aston Martin. It has the sort of stance on the road that makes it appear to have just kind of grown out of that particular spot on the tarmac. And it is beautifully balanced, its hugely powerful flanks countered by wings that lunge forward to a grille that looks ready to swallow the nearest Buick whole.

The last time I saw a Vanquish it was on a feather-dustered static display, every speck of lint carefully removed by white-gloved minders. It didn't seem real.

This is real. My kind of real; over the next few days, I'll be riding shotgun in the Vanquish as it makes it's way on what is, effectively, one lap of America. The journey started in Detroit, we'll ride along as far as New Orleans and the Vanquish will then continue west to Los Angeles before doubling back to Detroit via Denver.

I'll be riding with Dave Brassington on the first stint. Dave is an Aston Martin project manager, responsible for the multi-media systems on board the car. That's things like the sat nav, radio and mobile phone. He also knows every inch of the beast, which is why he has been tasked with this mammoth drive. And this particular Aston has been built on a mix of production and non-production tooling – it's called a second production proveout – and is just about 100 per cent production spec, mechanically. The interior, though, is not quite the cabin that a customer with £158,000 will get; those round vents will become rectangular on the production model and the switchgear will be arranged a little differently.

The idea behind this drive is that Dave and other engineers who'll join him – different groups swap over every couple of days – will drive the car as customers would, looking for any potential last minute problems. They are in daily communication with headquarters and Dave tells me that Ulrich Bez, Aston's chief executive, takes an extremely keen interest in even the most minor details of the Vanquish's progress. So the boss is watching.

The rain lets up, then the fog rolls in as we try to get clear of Atlanta. I've made myself comfortable, snuggled down into the passenger seat and powered it as far back as it will go. It feels snug but spacious enough in here, although the footwell ends at a near perpendicular angle that makes getting your feet comfortable a bit tricky. No quarrels about the generosity of the elbow room though, as Dave and I lounge expansively. Which is nice because we're both at the large end of the scale. Soon, we settle into a long-legged lope on highway 20 west.

A man with gold teeth floats up alongside in an ancient Chevrolet Cavalier. He's thrilled, barely able to control his car between wild thumbs-up and violent shakes of head. Near as I can tell, he's yelling "Daah-ham!" Americans like the Vanquish. A lot. It's growing on me, too. So far, Dave hasn't uncorked the 460bhp V12, choosing instead to cruise the car in automatic mode. In top gear, at a tall 34.9mph per thousand rpm, the Vanquish is smooth and refined, producing a gentle, distant growl hinting at the engine's other persona.

QUICK FACTS

Model	Aston Martin Vanquish
Price	£158,000
On sale	June 2001
0–60mph	4.5sec
0–100mph	10.0sec
Top speed	190mph-plus

FEATURE

18 APRIL 2001

Volume 228

No 3 I 5430

ABOVE NASCAR
action at Talladega Super
Speedway sees 400bhp
cars; Vanquish tops this
with another 60bhp.

OPPOSITE Vanquish is
equally at home cruising
the highway, or powering
through twists and turns
of mountain roads.

The transmission takes some getting used to, though. Even the engineers admit that your average Aston customer is going to need a little re-education; just like the nearly identical Magnetti Marelli system in the paddle-shift Ferrari F360 Modena, the Vanquish driveline is, effectively, a manual clutch system that can be shifted automatically with the help of a hydraulic pump and some nifty software. But because a clutch still needs to be depressed, there's a break in the torque flow as that happens. And around town at moderate speeds, that long pause between gears is very noticeable. To someone unclear about the concept – or more used to Lexus-like seamless shifting – it feels like an automatic that isn't working properly, creating inordinately long pauses between upshifts. There's a huge payback, though, as I'll shortly discover.

The man at Talladega Super Speedway doesn't seem that moved until I mention 'new Aston Martin Vanquish'.

Without blinking, he picks up the radio and informs whoever's on the other end that we are coming onto the circuit for a picture session. This is

where the NASCAR boys run, a four-corner bowl that holds the record for the fastest-ever NASCAR lap set by a Ford T-Bird at an average 212.809mph back in 1987. These days, they average just over 190mph, running on restricted power that my man

LIFE AS A VANQUISH

This particular Aston Martin Vanquish will have a short but glorious life. Code number SCFAC 13332 was built five months ago on a mix of production and prototype tooling. That said, the mechanical and software specifications on the car are up to full production British-spec standard. Before embarking on this trip, our Vanquish completed more than 5000 miles of testing in the Arctic conditions of Timmins, Ontario. There are now 9000 miles on the clock, with another 4000 to go before the car is returned to the UK, where it will be used as a donor car for other Aston projects, meaning that its life as a Vanquish will have lasted little more than six months.

reckons is just about 400bhp. I suggest that the Aston can top all of those figures right here, right now. At which point we are asked to leave.

And then, the finest piece of road I've ever encountered in the US of A. It twists and winds its way south from the Cheaha Mountain through Shinbone Valley and on to Montgomery, Alabama. And there is just about nobody on it, which is good because Dave is demonstrating a bit of payback. As soon as your start using the long paddles on the steering column to shift down or up, the Aston goes into manual mode, which is really quite glorious. We punch down from a sedate sixth gear to second in a blink – Aston reckons gear changes happen in less than 250 milliseconds – and the Vanquish responds with a brutal but perfectly matched spike of revs. Dave is wide open on the throttle and my neck muscles tense against the strain as those huge 285/40 Yokohamas fight for, and find, enormous grip. The engine note, previously a gently muted growl, hardens into a barrel-chested, bassy rebel yell. It's vaguely Italianate and quite wonderful.

I capture a good five minutes worth of this action on tape, Dave grabbing first and second near the top of the rev range, the downshifts with absolutely perfectly matched revs and the Aston shifting up a gear on its own accord if Dave leaves it a bit too late. Playing it back later on, I swear it would be impossible to tell whether this was a fully manual car being brilliantly driven, or the very clever machinations of the Marelli paddle-shift. When it works well, it works superbly. But there are compromises.

Rolling through town again, the Vanquish is less happy than it was playing up around the rev limiter. Spend any time at all sitting in traffic and the Aston will beep a warning to you, telling you that it has selected neutral to protect the clutch. It's difficult to remember this, so you find yourself unprepared when the light finally goes green. And because first gear is very tall, close-quarter low-speed manoeuvring soon provokes the acrid aroma of burning clutch. Owners expecting the total ease of a fully automatic box will have to get used

'PUNCH DOWN THROUGH THE GEARS AND THE ASTON RESPONDS WITH A BRUTAL SPIKE OF REVS'

ABOVE The only hint of power available from the V12 engine on the highway is a muted growl.

OPPOSITE Manual mode is glorious – Aston reckons gear changes happen in less than 250 milliseconds.

to these matters. But find that mountain road and all will be forgiven.

Another revelation comes as the Aston makes ground and we begin our approach to Mobile on Alabama's Gulf coast. We must be in a poor county because the roads are appalling and Dave isn't pussyfooting. Every time the Vanquish drops a big boot into yet another small crater, I stare at the dash, the A-pillar, anything for a hint of torsional flaccidity. Nothing. The car feels incredibly stiff, a fine testament to its extruded aluminium monocoque construction.

Which means the suspension can do its best work; in spite of its great girth – the Aston weighs a huge 1835kg – the car changes direction with a nimbleness you just wouldn't credit. The power-assisted steering is quickish at 2.7 turns lock to lock, and it is variably assisted, getting meatier at higher speeds. If Dave was feeling the weight under big brakes or into particularly tight twists, he wasn't

saying. And the integrity of the structure also helps the Vanquish to a very good ride quality for a car with such a sporting brief; the Yokohamas transmit ridges and surface changes, but there is very little noise when the suspension works, and no nervous jitters or tramlining. The best thing I can say of the Vanquish is that I emerged fresh and happy after a good eight-hour stint. Which is a mighty fine accomplishment for any car, much less a sub-five seconds to 60mph supercar.

We finish the photoshoot with the USS *Alabama* and head west out of Mobile. New Orleans is a good few hours away and we agree to head straight for the French quarter. The good bit. And it's Friday night.

We roll on to Bourbon Street just after 8pm. The place is absolutely heaving with a mostly friendly, mostly sober crowd. Reaction? I'm quite serious when I say that Britney Spears riding a unicycle wouldn't have had such an ecstatic

'A MAN WITH GOLD TEETH FLOATS UP ALONGSIDE. NEAR AS I CAN TELL, HE'S YELLING "DAAH-HAM!"'

reception. Even those who have no idea what an Aston Martin is are blown away. Which is why the Aston is reduced to a very slow creep, shrink-wrapped in the adoring crowd. Which might possibly have something to do with what happens next.

Dave goes for first gear, gets nothing. The Vanquish is stranded, gearless in the middle of a surging mob of happy Americans.

We push it to the safety of a quiet side street which turns out to be not so quiet. Women make breathtaking offers on the strength of our connection with the Vanquish. Men offer to help fix the problem which appears to be the hydraulic pump. A man dressed in a sequinned Raider T-shirt, a striped bandanna, jeans and a .45 Smith and Wesson turns out to be a cop. Makes an arrest, says 'nice car', leaves.

Dave and the boys fix the Aston in the hotel parking garage. No big deal, and when the trip's over, the faulty pump will be tested to destruction back at base to determine the cause of the failure.

As I leave, the guys are doing standing starts around the top floor of the garage. Just to make sure everything is cool.

And, of course, it is.

SPECIFICATIONS VANQUISH

ECONOMY

Urban	na
Extra urban	na
Combined	16.9mpg

DIMENSIONS

Length	4665mm
Width	1923mm
Height	1318mm
Wheelbase	2690mm
Weight	1835kg
Fuel tank	80 litres

ENGINE

Layout	12 cyls in vee, 5935cc
Max power	460bhp at 6500rpm
Max torque	400lb ft at 5000rpm
Specific output	77bhp per litre
Power to weight	255bhp per tonne
Installation	Front, longitudinal, rwd
Bore/stroke	89/79.5mm
Made of	Alloy
Compression ratio	10.5:1
Valve gear	4 per cyl, dohc
Ignition and fuel	Visteon twin PTEC engine management controlling ignition and fuel injection

SUSPENSION

Front Double wishbones, coils, anti-roll bar
Rear Double wishbones, coils, anti-roll bar

GEARBOX

Type Six-speed manual gearbox with ASM (Automatic Shift Manual) electro-hydraulic control
Ratios/mph per 1000rpm
Final drive ratio 3.69

1st 2.66/8.2	**2nd** 1.78/12.3
3rd 1.30/16.8	**4th** 1.00/21.9
5th 0.79/27.3	**6th** 0.63/34.9

STEERING

Type Rack and pinion, variable assist
Turns lock-to-lock 2.7 turns

BRAKES

Front 355mm ventilated, cross-drilled discs
Rear 330mm ventilated, cross-drilled discs

WHEELS AND TYRES

Size 9Jx19in (front), 10Jx19in (rear)
Made of Alloy
Tyres 255/40 ZR19 (f), 285/40 ZR19 (r)

THE **AUTOCAR** VERDICT

A true grand touring machine, but ultimate levels of driver involvement await that crucial first drive. Very promising.

All figures are manufacturer's claims

ASTON VANQUISH

The immensely capable Vanquish is a revelation, and is already proving to be Britain's finest supercar since the McLaren F1

The DB7, you will remember, is the car that saved Aston Martin. It was fast and beautiful but had to play it straight down the middle to a clientele who bought it for that most traditional of reasons: because they wanted an Aston. Without it, the company would not exist today.

By contrast the all-new £158,000 Vanquish was conceived for different reasons and different people. The company is safe, so it bears no burden of necessity on its shoulders. It can afford to be more wildly liberating, expensive and daring than a DB7. This is the car Aston Martin wanted to build, not one it had to build. It's appeal is not simply steeped in the marque's heritage, but is rather one to compete on the world stage and steal the sales from Bentley, Porsche and Ferrari.

So while you'll find the skeleton of an XJS inside a DB7, in the Vanquish there are aerospace construction techniques. Where wood once ruled the cabin, now there is polished aluminium. And while the exterior may resemble the DB7, conceptually and technologically it is the biggest step forward Aston has taken since the introduction of the DB4 in 1959.

QUICK FACTS

Model tested	Vanquish
List price	£158,000
Top speed	196mph (see text)
30–70mph	3.7sec
0–60mph	4.4sec
60–0mph	3.0sec
MPG	12.6
For	Engine and gearbox, steering, ride, looks, quality
Against	Brake fade, cabin lacks atmosphere, poor fuel range

ROAD TEST

8 AUGUST 2001

Volume 229
No 6 | 5446

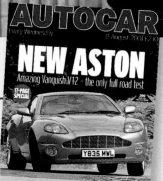

AUTOCAR
Every Wednesday
8 August 2001 £2.10

NEW ASTON
Amazing Vanquish V12 – the only full road test
17-PAGE SPECIAL

Y835 MWL

WORLD EXCLUSIVE
The car that will rebuild Rover

Y267 DBW

ROAD TEST VANQUISH

ACCELERATION FROM REST

True mph	seconds	speedo mph
30	2.0	30
40	2.8	40
50	3.6	50
60	4.4	60
70	5.7	71
80	7.3	82
90	8.6	92
100	10.5	103
110	12.3	114
120	14.3	125
130	17.0	136
140	19.8	147
150	22.6	159

Standing qtr mile 13.3sec/115mph
Standing km 22.9sec/151mph
30-70mph through gears 3.7sec

ACCELERATION IN GEAR

MPH	6th	5th	4th	3rd	2nd
20–40	-	9.8	8.2	4.0	2.4
30–50	10.4	9.1	4.8	3.3	2.4
40–60	10.4	5.6	4.6	3.3	2.4
50–70	8.4	5.8	4.4	3.3	2.4
60–80	8.2	6.1	4.4	3.2	2.4
70–90	8.2	6.3	4.7	3.1	2.6
80–100	9.3	6.4	4.8	3.4	-
90–110	9.9	6.7	4.8	3.4	-
100–120	10.8	7.2	4.7	-	-
110–130	11.4	7.4	4.9	-	-
120–140	11.7	7.8	5.5	-	-
130–150	13.7	8.2	6.0	-	-

MAXIMUM SPEEDS

6th	196mph/5610rpm	5th	191/7000
4th	153/7000	3rd	118/7000
2nd	86/7000	1st	57/7000

FUEL CONSUMPTION

Average/best/worst/touring
12.6/20.8/5.5/20.8mpg

Urban/combined	na/16.9mpg
Tank capacity	80 litres
Touring range	366 miles
CO$_2$	396g/km

BRAKES

30/50/70mph	9.6/27.7/51.1 metres
60–0mph	2.9sec

NOISE

Idle/max revs in 3rd 52/90dbA
30/50/70mph 67/69/75dbA

TESTER'S NOTES

- Insiders at Aston hate the red starter button but the Yanks love it apparently. Because the US is the car's biggest market, it stuck.
- The rear screen brake light is to be moved from its current position to the top of the rear screen. Which is good news because it obstructs vision badly at the moment.
- Car looks better on the road than it does on a showstand. Much better.

DESIGN AND ENGINEERING ★★★★
Cutting edge technology bring new dimension to Aston design

For once, beauty is considerably more than skin deep and you need to look at the core of the Vanquish to discover the depth of engineering quality it enjoys.

There you will find a central supporting structure doubling as the transmission tunnel, crafted from carbon fibre. Around this are bonded and riveted sections of extruded aluminium upon which hand-finished aluminium body panels are hung. The A-pillars are carbon fibre too. The result is a massively strong and torsionally rigid platform.

Its task is to cope with the same 5.9-litre V12 engine in the DB7 Vantage, but fettled with new uprated camshafts, manifolds and a revised crankshaft and valve-gear to provide a nominal 460bhp at 6500rpm and an unchanged torque figure of 400lb ft at 5000rpm.

This urge is directed rearwards through the same six-speed manual gearbox found in the DB7 and

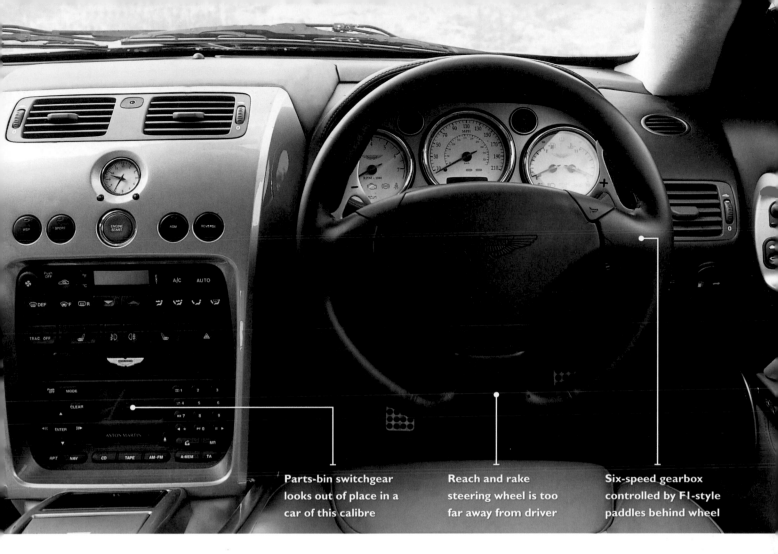

Parts-bin switchgear looks out of place in a car of this calibre

Reach and rake steering wheel is too far away from driver

Six-speed gearbox controlled by F1-style paddles behind wheel

Chrysler Viper, but thanks to work by Ford and Magneti-Marelli, it does without a clutch pedal and is electronically actuated via paddles on the steering wheel.

From there the power is fed through a limited-slip differential to the tarmac via bespoke Yokohama AVS tyres. As befits its performance potential, these boots are vast 285/40 ZR19 affairs adorning 10in wide forged rear wheels and scarcely thinner 255/40s up front, reflecting the weight of that engine in the nose. Switchable traction control is standard.

Beautifully machined aluminium wishbones form the basis of the suspension at each corner while huge ventilated discs (355mm up front, 330 at the rear) provide the stopping power, abetted by a Teves anti-lock system.

The Ian Callum-designed body retains aluminium wings and while volume and efficiency requirements mean they are no longer beaten by hand, each is still finished manually, preserving the sound and history of hammers hitting metal at Newport Pagnell for a while yet.

The Vanquish benefits from a test programme fully commensurate with the demands of the 21st century, with over 50 prototypes racking up one million miles of testing in Canada and Australia. Chassis development benefited from a broad pool of talent: Aston's own engineers worked with others from within its Ford parent (up to and including product vice-president, Richard Parry-Jones) and also from Lotus Engineering.

PERFORMANCE AND BRAKES ★★★★
Superb performance, although brakes are disappointing

It is clear from your first full-throttle moments in the Vanquish this is much quicker than the DB7 Vantage; what is rather less obvious given a less than 10 per cent power increase and no great difference in kerb weight is why this should be. So whatever the reason, the DB is extremely quick, the Vanquish plays a different tune altogether.

With Millbrook unavailable we reverted to the runway at Bruntingthorpe to record performance figures, a location offering a pale shadow of the

ABOVE Hand-me-down dials/controls look out of place in otherwise bespoke interior that is spacious for two.

OPPOSITE Starter button and clock give dash a retro feel; supportive seats and long gearing make for a civilised touring companion in a car of rare ability.

WHAT IT COSTS

ASTON MARTIN VANQUISH

On-the-road price	£158,000
Price as tested	£163,870
Cost per mile	na
CO$_2$	396g/km

INSURANCE

Insurance/typical quote	20/£1669

WARRANTY

24 months/unlimited miles, 6 years rust

SERVICING

Full service every 7500 miles or 12 months

EQUIPMENT CHECKLIST

Air conditioning	■
Traction control	■
Leather trim	■
Electric front seats	■
Satellite navigation	**£2109**
Height/tilt-adjust steering	■/■
Anti-lock brakes	■
Airbag driver/passenger/side	■/■/-
RDS stereo/CD player	■/■
Alarm/immobiliser	■/■

Options in **bold** fitted to test car
■ = Standard na = not available

BELOW Firmer ride and monumental grip makes the Vanquish the best handling production Aston in history.

traction offered by Millbrook's high-grip surface. Despite this and a gearchange that doesn't swap cogs in less than the blink of the eye, it still blasted to 60mph in 4.4sec and 100mph in 10.5sec. had we been able to use Millbrook and change gear ourselves, these figures would have been closer to

4.1sec and 9.5sec. As it is, the Vanquish is every bit as quick as the Ferrari 550 Maranello (4.6sec/10.1sec) it rivals.

Better still, it does all this while bellowing the unique howl of the high performance V12 into your ears, a song Ferrari appears to have forgotten. So inspirational is this tune it highlights even more the slight but still irksome pause between upshifts. Coming down the gearbox is a much more delightful task: flick the paddle the appropriate number of times and it will drop as many ratios as you wish in one snarling blip of the throttle.

The shift quality up or down is always smooth – even when you select automatic via a dashboard switch. The entire gearbox installation and application can be described as a success and something approaching a triumph when you consider the 'box started life in a truck.

Simply leaving it in third gear copes with almost every situation the open road can throw at you from walking pace to 120mph. Unlike Ferrari, Aston Martin has chosen super-wide gear ratios for the Vanquish so that if you select fourth and let the V12 do its stuff, you'll be doing over 160mph before it

screams into its rev limiter at 7200rpm. So while the Ferrari needs every rev it has to reach its 199mph top speed in sixth gear, the Vanquish tops out in fifth. Were it to reach its red line in sixth it would be with over 250mph on the clock. We were able to reach over 175mph with childish ease within the confines of Bruntingthorpe's runway, its claimed 190mph plus maximum is conservative.

How disappointing, therefore, to discover brakes that felt and proved unequal to such performance standards. The discs may be enormous but that comes as little reassurance when pedal travel is disconcertingly long, the feel is spongy and the 60–0mph time of 2.9sec is slower than that of vastly more modest cars.

Sure, this 1835kg car is no lightweight, and some allowance should be made for the compromised surface, and doubtless we asked more of its brakes in testing. But the procedure is the same for all cars and, bluntly, the brakes offered, at best, only mediocre performance.

HANDLING AND RIDE ★★★★★
Brilliant chassis provides near perfect ride/handling balance

Behind the headlines grabbed by that sublime engine and smart gearbox lies a chassis of less obvious but not less impressive ability. For the Vanquish to work it would need to do more than look good and go hard – Astons have always had a firm grip on those disciplines – it would need to enthral, reward, comfort and keep safe the serious enthusiast driver, and that means top-drawer handling.

It succeeds in spades. Your first few yards confirm that, for all its new found sportiness, this Aston rides as well as a DB7. It's firmer but so fluent is the damping and so well does it maintain its ride height on the most undulating roads that what little (if any) it gives away in secondary absorption, it more than counters with primary body control. This is reassuring, as is the perfectly judged weight of the rack and pinion steering, and the combined pitch is so convincing it makes you want to drive the car hard from the outset.

Doing so reveals the best handling car Aston has

ever produced; although in truth, that is not quite the accolade it should be. Its handling can hold its head high even beside the 550 Maranello, a multiple winner of our handling day contest. It offers similar levels of grip and traction and perhaps even better steering feel.

Under race-track loadings, the Ferrari's almost absurdly accommodating nature provides a greater range of on-limit options, but no one is going to quibble with the Vanquish's mild understeer into the apex or the tail-out drift to the exit that can be provoked with a stab of the right foot and the traction control disabled.

In the real world, such issues are irrelevant. It points with a rare precision for one so heavy, hits its marks every time and slingshots away from corners with an alacrity once the preserve of mid- and rear-engined cars. Occasionally a politely flashing light lets you know the traction control is trimming the worst excesses from your driving, but it is unobtrusive so it's best to let it get on with it.

ABOVE Maintains ride height over almost any road surface.

'THE VANQUISH IS THE CAR ASTON MARTIN WANTED TO BUILD, NOT ONE IT HAD TO BUILD'

SPECIFICATIONS VANQUISH

DIMENSIONS

Min/max front legroom 910/1100mm Min/max front headroom 850/900mm
Min/max rear legroom 410/600mm Kerb weight 1835kg Boot volume 170/litres/dm³
Min/max boot width 870/1260mm Boot height 580mm Boot length 960mm
Front/rear tracks 1572/1584mm Width (including mirrors) 1998mm

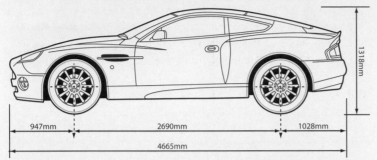

1318mm

947mm   2690mm   1028mm

4665mm

ENGINE

Layout	12 cyls in vee, 5925cc
Max power	460bhp at 6500rpm
Max torque	400lb ft at 5000rpm
Specific output	78bhp per litre
Power to weight	251bhp per tonne
Torque to weight	218lb ft per tonne
Installation	Longitudinal, front, rear-wheel drive
Construction	Alloy heads & block
Bore/stroke	89.0/79.5mm
Valve gear	4 per cyl, dohc
Compression ratio	10.5:1
Management	Visteon Twin PTEC engine management system, sequential fuel injection

TRANSMISSION

Gearbox 6-speed manual with Automatic Shift Manual (ASM)
Ratios/mph per 1000rpm
Final drive 3.69

1st 2.66/8.2	2nd 1.78/12.3
3rd 1.30/16.8	4th 1.00/21.9
5th 0.79/27.3	6th 0.63/34.9

STEERING

Type Rack and pinion, variable power assisted
Turns lock-to-lock 2.7
Turning circle 11.7m

CHASSIS AND BODY

Body	Two-door coupé, Cd 0.35
Wheels	Alloy 9Jx19in (f), 10Jx19in (r)
Tyres	255/40 ZR19 (f), 285/40 ZR19 (r)
	Yokohama AV S Sport
Spare	Emergency puncture kit

SUSPENSION

Front Double wishbones, coil springs, damper, anti-roll bar
Rear Double wishbones, coil springs, dampers, anti-roll bar

BRAKES

Front 355mm ventilated, cross-drilled discs
Rear 330mm ventilated, cross-drilled discs
Anti-lock Standard

But for all it's grip and composure, there is no escaping the Vanquish is a heavy car and, unsurprisingly, feels it. Expect Lotus Elise levels of steering feel and you will be disappointed; expect it to change direction mid-corner like a scrum-half and you will end up in the hedge. The engineers at Aston, Ford and Lotus are as good as they come, but they cannot rewrite the laws of physics.

ECONOMY ★★
Awful consumption and small tank seriously compromise range

We achieved an overall fuel consumption of 12.6mpg, with a best of 20.8mpg and a worst of 5.5mpg. Ghastly though such figures sound, even if trundling owners manage 15mpg, the Vanquish's range on its 80-litre tank is under 250 miles. Cruise across Europe in style and at the speeds at which the Vanquish is at its effortless best, and you'll need to start looking for service stations at roughly hourly intervals.

SAFETY AND EQUIPMENT ★★★
Interior quality no match for price, but refinement is first rate

The delay in launching the Vanquish was worth it, particularly as now the interior not only looks better, but it is also a roomier, more comfortable place to be. The driving position is reasonable, though many will find the steering wheel too far away despite being both reach and rake adjustable, while a potentially cramped pedal box is perfectly adequate thanks to the omission of a clutch pedal.

Sadly, however, the Vanquish's interior is still one we struggle to equate with a car of this price. Sit in a 550 Maranello and every switch, knob, dial and control feels and appears bespoke; sit in the Vanquish and while individual items look up to snuff in isolation – the diamond pattern seat leather, headlining, monikered aluminium grab handles and elegant instruments to name a few – the overall effect smacks too heavily of parts bin dependency. Most out of place is the entire centre console which has been lifted wholesale from Jaguar's XJ saloon – and it didn't look that great in a car costing less than a quarter of the price of this Aston.

But at least the Vanquish is now sufficiently roomy for two tall adults while the sensibly shaped boot should swallow enough luggage to obviate the need to plan touring holidays with military precision. Better still, save yourself about £6000 and don't specify the almost utterly useless rear seats, and give over a space that is not really fit for human occupation to even more luggage.

In touring guise, the Vanquish is a splendid companion. Long gearing, soft but supportive seats, excellent sound suppression and that oh-so-impressive ride produce a sports car of rare civility.

Only on exceptionally coarse and usually concrete surfaces do those huge Yokohamas kick up intrusive levels of tyre roar while wind noise — an old DB7 bugbear — at all speeds up to and including the truly insane, is admirably muted.

Aston Martin is exceptionally proud of the Vanquish's crash-worthiness, much of it mapped out on computers before any were rammed into walls, but, of course, we're not able to verify these claims. Certainly, the evident rigidity of the chassis and presence of composite crash structure front and rear, point to strong passive safety, while on-board equipment includes traction control, anti-lock, twin air-bags and side impact beams as well as a tyre pressure sensing system.

Other equipment includes the usual goodies such as leather, electric seats, climate control, automatic headlights and wipers and a modest trip computer. Satellite navigation is an optional extra.

AUTOCAR VERDICT

Aston Martin had done it. The DB7 pulled the company from the brink and the Vanquish has moved the game on again — now it can truly claim to rival Ferrari. Which, of course, it would not do, believing that it has no rivals. Even so, there is no better way we can describe the Vanquish and no praise more lavish that we can heap upon it than to say, in almost all ways, it is a credible alternative to a 550 Maranello. Subjectively it sounds better and objectively it goes as hard; technologically it is cleverer and is prettier — on the outside at least.

We have reservations about the interior, brakes, fuel range and, some reliability doubts. But these in no way diminish the scale of the Vanquish's achievement. It is Aston's best effort yet and Britain's finest supercar this side of a McLaren F1.

Best Aston ever is a brilliant GT ★★★★

MARKET & FINANCE ★★★★★
Huge demand, tiny supply should ensure strong residuals

An instantly appealing shape, a badge to die for and the pent up demand for a British Ferrari-chaser means even at £158,000 the Vanquish looks like a car born to cling to its residuals. This will be helped by the news that all 500 Vanquishes to be built this year and next have already found homes and that the waiting list stretches through 2003.

BELOW Extremely rigid platform ensures Vanquish is a safe and entertaining handler for such a heavy car.

20:20 VISION

GIUGIARO TWENTY TWENTY As the Vanquish is readied for launch, Giugiaro casts a fresh eye on the DB7. *By Peter Robinson*

Here's a surprise. Giugiaro, father and son, decided to design a beautiful car – nothing more, nothing less – for this year's Geneva Show. Beauty above all would be the justification for this concept car's existence.

And Giorgetto and Fabrizio created a striking open-top two-seater. It didn't being life as an Aston Martin, but, in the end, appeared on Giugiaro's Italdesign Geneva stand as the Aston Twenty Twenty, just metres away from Aston's gorgeous new Vanquish. Which only made the inevitable comparision more telling.

Despite the forlorn hope, the Twenty Twenty is not beautiful. Individual, unique, distinctive, yes, but not beautiful.

Twenty Twenty – the name was suggested by Aston's new boss Ulrich Bez, not Giugiaro – continues Italdesign's fascination with an exposed light-alloy structure. The aluminium skeleton of the Twenty Twenty, first seen on its 1998 Structura, becomes a design feature. Trouble is, it introduces a fussy, if striking, two-tone effect that only emphasises the heaviness of the car's appearance.

"Last year, we did 30 full-scale models for clients," says Fabrizio Giugiaro, "and by September my father and I wondered if we would even go to Geneva. Finally, we decided to so something hedonistic and beautiful. When we do intelligent cars, no one appreciates the design.

"Our idea was to mix a classically beautiful design, something strong, with technology that shows off our engineering skills and combines the exposed space frame with the hedonistic style. In the beginning it was just a concept, it wasn't close to any particular brand and neutral. My father wanted to do it alone as a Giugiaro concept. We thought there was no badge stronger than ours, that people would say it's a typical Giugiaro design."

The story of how the Twenty Twenty came to be an Aston Martin says something about the complex and delicate politics of a huge multi-national

FEATURE

8 AUGUST 2001

Volume 229

No 6 | 5446

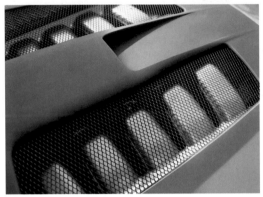

ABOVE Lacquered veneer and aluminium dominate interior; aluminium skeleton becomes a design detail in its own right.

OPPOSITE Complex surfaces give a heavy look.

car maker. Naturally, Ulrich Bez, an old friend of the Giugiaros, was involved – (during his five years as head of R&D at Daewoo, Bez and the Giugiaros created a number of Daewoo models, most notably the Matiz).

As the new broom at Aston, he was frustrated to discover that the company only ever asked Ian Callum (who styled both the DB7 and Vanquish) to style its cars, and wanted to get some fresh ideas for future Aston looks, so asked Giugiaro to design a car for Geneva.

"I could only give them an old V12 DB7 chassis and running gear, a car we would have crashed. The rest was up to Giugiaro. It had to be clear it was a Giugiaro project and not an official Aston Martin concept."

Bez first saw the unnamed concept car in October. "We told him he could have this idea," says Fabrizio Giugiaro. "He told us to make it as close to an Aston as possible. He knows it could be made for anybody, or it could be an Aston Martin.

"He knew what we needed to do, it was like he'd been at Aston for 20 years. We wanted to catch the Aston character. We added the vent behind the front wheel arch, created a fender line over the rear wheel arch and an Aston Martin grille."

"It's difficult for Italians to do an Aston Martin," admits Giugiaro Jnr. "The Twenty Twenty fights with the elegant Vanquish. We wanted a Vanquish chassis,

but it was too new and is a different project, so we had to keep the DB7 platform.

"We believe in the visible space-frame. We knew some would like the design and some would not."

Callum, playing the diplomat, prefers not to comment, though he (and Ford design boss J Mays) saw the Twenty Twenty through its styling development. Would the car, which is longer and has more overhang and greater width than a DB7, look lighter, more handsome and less brutal if it were painted one colour so that the space frame didn't confuse the eye? Fabrizio admits the alloy sections could be painted body colour. Anything to reduce the weight of those sills.

"Its completely different (in one colour), but doesn't give the feeling of the material. We wanted to be able to touch the alloy, to feel it."

Inside, however, the superbly finished soft leather, lacquered veneer and aluminium design is a realistic approach to a modern Aston. It's simple, elegant and more spacious than a DB7, even if the seats are mounted too high. A pair of "emergency" seats are hidden under a tonneau-like leather cover. From behind the wheel, few people will notice the concept car retains the DB7's windscreen. The screen of Giorgetto's sketches was so close to the DB7 they decided to retain the original. "Mays liked the interior," says Giugiaro, "He was neutral about the exterior, but wanted us to go ahead."

Look beyond the styling and it's a six-speed DB7. Twenty Twenty presents advanced technology because the panels are bonded to the spaceframe, Giugiaro says they could be made of alloy, carbon fibre or plastic, or even small sheet-steel sections. That means any client taking up the exposed spaceframe idea could use different panels to produce a variety of models in small-scale production.

Italdesign has made sure the Twenty Twenty drives, although when we took it out it tramlined badly and vibrated at 75mph. Blame out-of-balance 20in BBS wheels. Still, Fabrizio has driven it across Europe to Aston's HQ at Newport Pagnell and it was shipped to Detroit for the annual Eyes on Design show in June, including the 1000-miles Eyes on the Road event.

"I wanted to use the car for my holidays in America," says the younger Giugiaro. "It was born as a roadster, but with the targa-top we can close the roof (the panel sits neatly in the boot when the car's open) and with the standard suspension it's very comfortable. It's a prototype, but for a touring drive it's perfect."

Talk to Giugiaro about the Aston and the subject of Ferrari comes up. You get the impression that Italdesign would love one of its proposals to be chosen as a Ferrari production car. Despite competing for various projects, Maranello continues to prefer Pininfarina, Ferrari's traditional coachbuilder.

Will the Twenty Twenty contribute to the appearance of future Aston Martins? I doubt it, despite Bez's keenness to look beyond the Callum-box. Fabrizio is one of the most pleasant of motor industry people. I count him a friend. Will he still talk to me if I say his latest car isn't close to being beautiful? I wouldn't got so far as to call it ugly, but it's close.

'THE TWENTY TWENTY IS NOT BEAUTIFUL. INDIVIDUAL, UNIQUE AND DISTINCTIVE, YES, BUT NOT BEAUTIFUL'

MOUTH & TROUSERS

DB7 ZAGATO Sensuous lines and gaping grille courtesy of Italy's Zagato, 450bhp V12 and weight saving by Aston. Result? A brilliant sign-off for the DB7. *By Steve Cropley*

For the third time in its proud, chequered post-war history, Aston Martin has joined forces with Zagato, the legendary Milanese coachbuilder, to produce a special-bodied two-seater GT. This time it's the DB7 Zagato, a car that will emphasise the bespoke exclusivity of the marque and give the current DB7 an extra fillip towards the end of its life.

The new car, which uses the ordinary DB7 chassis and lightly tweaked running gear, has an all-new shape. It neatly combines influences from the original Zagato-bodied Aston DB4 GT of 1960 with more recent Zagato-designed concept cars, and mixes in contemporary Aston references from both the DB7 and Vanquish. The result is a rare, pretty and delicate-looking coach-built car whose key virtue is that final assembly can take place alongside existing DB7s at Bloxham, near Banbury.

Over the past few weeks Aston Martin people have been showing the prototype to potential buyers and 'gauging reaction'. So far those likely prospects have been bullish, says Aston. The company plans to build between 75 and 99 DB7 Zagatos, priced at £160,000 "plus or minus five per cent", but the final decision won't be made for a week or two. However, Aston's willingness to reveal the car now makes a go-ahead look like a formality. Production should begin next March, and soon reach a rate of five a week, so it should conclude before the end of 2003.

The DB7 Zagato has come to life at amazing speed. It is mostly the work of Zagato, but includes regular input from Henrik Fisker, Aston's British-based design chief. His key concern is that the new car should combine well with as-yet-unseen Astons in the pipeline, notably the next DB7 and the new small Aston, AM305. The idea for the DB7 Zagato sprang from a chance meeting between Aston's chief

executive, Ulrich Bez, and Andrea Zagato, the third generation head of his family's 83-year-old company, at the Pebble Beach concours in Santa Monica this time last year.

"Ulli and I were on the same judging panel," says Zagato. "We'd never met before, but we hit it off. The following day we got talking again, and the idea came up of our two companies doing another car together – something very much in the spirit of the previous models. We decided to explore the idea, and the whole thing has grown from there."

Within weeks, Aston and Zagato had agreed a brief for the new car that looked consistent with the two previous co-operative models, the 1960 DB4 GTZ and the 1986 Aston Martin Vantage Zagato. The car would have a shorter wheelbase than the existing DB7, plus shorter front and rear overhangs, wider tracks and a "more dynamic" rear end. Andrea Zagato came to the UK in December last year with initial sketches, to check that Bez, Fisker and their marketing experts were happy with the project's direction.

In February, Aston dispatched a normal DB7 to Zagato to be the basis of a prototype, and at the same time Zagato produced a firm rendering of how he thought the car should look. Then, in March this year, at Geneva show time, Zagato entertained the whole Aston team in Milan, presented computer renderings of the proposed new model – which their CAD designs had already proven to be feasible – and in a four-hour meeting the whole thing was approved.

Over the following three months, the running prototype in our photographs was built and commissioned. It arrived in Britain in June. Since then, Aston has been assessing the car for its production process, and showing it to customers. One gathering was at the tailors, Gieves & Hawkes – No 1 Savile Row

'A BREATHTAKING CAR, AND AMAZINGLY DIFFERENT FROM THE DB7 ITSELF, CONSIDERING THE HIDDEN SIMILARITIES'

AUTOCAR

Every Week

21 August 2002 £2.10

NEW ASTON DB7
EXCLUSIVE!

Our spies uncover 2004's
190mph super-Brit

PLUS Zagato's £170k
designer Aston

THIS WEEK
Vauxhall's
baby MPV driven
Speed cameras
– the hidden truth
Maserati Coupé tested

SHOCK! VOLVO'S
NEW OFF-ROADER
RATTLES BMW X5

Why XC90 is this year's must-have 4x4

ABOVE Raked fastback typically Zagato.

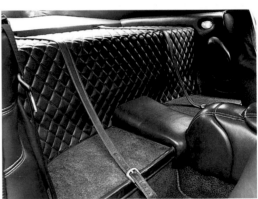

RIGHT Leather-lined interior mostly unchanged; Zagato loses DB7's rear seats.

OPPOSITE 450bhp and a weight reduction should see Zagato hit 185mph; tiny boot space.

– where the car stood among bespoke suits, and 120 prospective customers were encouraged to take in its exclusivity and hand-made appeal: in short, draw parallels between the car and the classily cut cloth around it.

Most of the the Zagato's underpinnings are standard DB7, except that the wheelbase is shortened by 60mm – which means the car loses the standard DB7's already impossibly cramped rear seats and becomes a pure two-seater. The inner structure must remain unaltered or expensive new crash tests would be necessary, impractical considering the Zagato's tiny production volume. The windscreen and scuttle are recognisable from the standard car and so are the faired-in headlights, but apart from that the new car's skin is all-new, much of it is aluminium: bonnet, doors, front wings and bootlid. The roof and rear wings, however, are steel and welded into place.

The complete car is 211mm shorter overall: 60mm saved in the wheelbase, 24mm from the front overhang and 127mm from the rear. The front track is 20mm wider, the rear 30mm, as a result of which the Zagato's body is around 30mm wider overall. Though the nose is hardly shorter it loses some bulk, and now features an aggressive egg-crate grille, reminiscent of the '60s DB4 Zagato, hand-crafted in aluminium. The body has Virage-like sinews and muscles running down its sides to a chopped Kamm tail featuring simple but beautifully executed round tail-lights. Same description fits the twin upswept tailpipes, one each side.

The main Zagato reference is in the grille and upper body: the side-glass shapes, the 'double-bubble' roof, and the fastback that's raked so radically it's almost flat. A breathtaking car, and amazingly different from the DB7 itself, considering the hidden similarities. The short tail leaves the car with a very small boot, accessible through a slot-like aperture so impractical that it usually raises a smile from potential customers. In fact, it's so close to a joke that Aston Martin's people see it as a sales aid: a car with a boot this silly has to be special. But they'll still do a roaring trade in fitted luggage.

The interior is little different from the standard DB7's, but areas such as the seat cushions have quilt-stitching, a neat reference to other bespoke Italian cars. The whole thing is trimmed in lacquer-free leather which looks more natural than usual, and adds value in the weakest area.

There are mechanical differences, too, but Aston Martin is still refining them. In production, the car will have slightly stiffer spring and damper rates than standard. It will also be lower-geared overall, using a 4.09 to one diff ratio, as opposed to the standard DB7 Vantage's 3.77. Overall gearing in top (sixth) gear will therefore fall from 32mph/1000rpm to around 29/1000, and by a similar percentage in other gears. The Zagato gets the same tyres as the Vantage: 245/40 ZR18s for the front and 265/35 ZR18s at the rear.

By tweaking the 5.9-litre V12 engine's fuelling electronics, Aston will give the car 20–30bhp more, pushing peak power close to 450bhp. Throw in the Zagato's shorter gearing and a weight saving estimated at 60kg (kerb weight is around 1740kg) and you should have a car that can turn in 0–60mph sprints in the high four-second bracket, a 0–100mph time close to the Vanquish's 10.5sec, and a top speed of about 185mph.

Some of the DB7 Zagato's steep looking £70,000 premium over the Vantage can be laid at the door of its exclusivity and style, but some more will be accounted for by the cumbersome logistics of its manufacture. Modified underframes will be shipped in from the UK to Zagato's works in Italy to be hand-fitted with outer panels, then the whole assembly will be returned to Bloxham for painting and final assembly on the DB7 line.

Design chief Fisker is ecstatic about the new car, which he believes has the lightness of the best cars of the '50s and '60s. "While everyone else is getting bigger and heavier, we're getting smaller and lighter," he says. "I like that a lot." The new DB7 is clearly a Zagato car, he adds, but it's still a good indicator of where Aston is heading.

"We'll have more cars like this, more special cars, alongside our new models. I hate it when people say you can't do great cars any more, because of all the current regulations. That's not true. We've got some fantastic stuff coming, and the rules won't stop us. And what's more, there won't be long to wait."

ZAGATO ASTONS

DB4 GT. Originally it was to be a one-off, built for Aston's Milan distributor who wanted a road car that could be raced. But Aston bosses liked it so much they adopted it as a special edition. Nineteen were built. With 314bhp and a 0–60mph time of about 5.5sec, the lighter-than-standard Zagato could give Ferrari GTOs a run on the track. It has become one of the most valuable Astons – and so rare that Aston and Zagato backed a project to build four more in 1991. Originals go for £1.5m, and a Sanction Two (as the '90s cars are called) recently sold for around £900,000.

The second model, the Vantage Zagato of 1986, helped Aston to cash in on a price boom for specialist cars. Victor Gauntlett, Aston's boss at the time, had seen Ferrari succeed brilliantly with the 288 GTO. At the Geneva Show in 1985, he and Gianni Zagato (Andrea's father) struck a deal whereby Aston took a stake in the coachbuilder while the model, based on the 5.3-litre V8 Vantage of the time, was built.

A production run of 75 cars was planned, but 87 were built: 57 coupés and 30 Volante convertibles. Many thought they didn't look sufficiently like a traditional Aston, and have never quite achieved the celebrity of their august predecessors.

PREMIUM BOND

JAMES BOND VANQUISH One crucial ingredient has been missing from 007's latest films: his Aston Martin Now it's back, packing the sort of kit you won't find in any dealer brochure. *By Ben Oliver*

If you go to see *Die Another Day* – the twentieth James Bond movie which opens next month – and find the experience utterly ruined when the idiot in front of you keeps pointing at the screen during the car chase sequences, nudging his mates and only half-whispering anoraky, know-it-all 'facts', then I apologise. That idiot will be an *Autocar* road tester. But I hope you'll forgive his misplaced enthusiasm; we've witnessed much of the making of the motorised bits of the latest Bond caper and are desperate to see the results.

It started in January this year. We arrived at the Chobham test track in Surrey, a place we use almost daily, pretty pleased to be driving the first.Lamborghini Murcielago in the country. It isn't a car you expect to be upstaged in, so we were choked to find James Bond's Aston Martin Vanquish and the Jaguar XKR convertible of his latest foe, the hideously scarred North Korean, Zao, being shaken down by the special effects team. Only later was it officially announced that Bond was ending his overlong affair with the products of a well-known Bavarian manufacturer and getting back into as British a motor as he could manage, short of a Morgan or a Noble. Ford's sponsorship deal didn't extend to putting the villain in something from General Motors or Chrysler, so Zao gets the Jag and the delectable Halle Berry, Bond's latest squeeze, gets a Ford Thunderbird.

Sadly, Halle never made it to Chobham, being fully occupied with the movie's principal photography which began at Pinewood at the same time. Sadly for her, you understand – I mean, what Hollywood starlet doesn't want to meet a bunch of unkempt, overweight road testers? Our egos, bruised at being upstaged in the Lambo and stood up by Halle, were slightly assuaged when one of the stunt drivers had an

almighty and most un-Bond-like accident in Zao's Jag, losing it on the black ice of a wintry Chobham and finding a concrete bollard which tore the front end off.

No risk of that in the next Bond vehicle we encountered. The story begins with a hovercraft chase through the demilitarised zone between North and South Korea. It will have to be pretty spectacular to beat the boat chase that opened *The World Is Not Enough* and doubtless will be, despite being filmed at the Army's Long Valley test area in bucolic Hampshire, where we do our off-road testing. We arrived feeling unassailable in the mighty new Range Rover, only to find ourselves surrounded by red stars and machine gun emplacements and beset by hovercraft powered by twin 600cc Rotax two-stroke engines piloted by blokes in combat gear which went and sounded like fury. The Range Rover just shrank.

And then, like all good Bond sagas, we found our way into the heart of the operation: Pinewood Studios, home to the Bond industry for most of its 40-year history. Aston wanted us to see – officially now – its car in action. But this rather naïve filmgoer was slightly disillusioned. You expect a major movie set to be immensely glamorous, but the interior of Zao's Icelandic ice palace, the scene for the day's filming, looked more like a cheap nightclub with the lights turned up – tacky and crudely done. More worryingly, once the scene had been reset a vast sprinkler system was turned on – the place is supposed to be melting as Bond and Zao chase each other around it – drenching everything, including us and the vast tangles of electrical cables powering the lights and cameras. I'd rather die another day too.

None of this fazed stuntman George Cottle, who at least had the benefit of a wetsuit under his costume. Only the Jag was in action in that scene

'THE ASTON MARTIN STARTS WITH A FEROCIOUS ROAR DESPITE BEING LIMITED TO A RATHER UNHEROIC 40MPH'

FEATURE

23 OCTOBER 2002

Volume 234

No 4 | 5508

AUTOCAR

50 EXTRA PAGES

MOTOR SHOW GUIDE 2002

New 150mph Fiesta

the reveal the hot Fiesta hot kms faster and the new lives muss

PLUS Bond is back.... and we've driven his new Aston

and George, his face made up to resemble Zao's diamond-scarred visage, had to pilot it behind a camera car in loops around the set, using its hydraulic handbrake to get it around some of the tighter corners. The car looked as bad as the set in its bright emerald green paintwork, but action unit director Vic Armstrong assured us that both would look sensational on celluloid. Vic was one of the world's top stuntmen in his day and directed that boat chase, so I'm sure we'll be impressed. But a worrying thought – what if Halle Berry doesn't look as fine in the flesh? We'll never know.

The Pinewood workshops probably had more Vanquishes than the Aston factory. Seven were supplied, three 'hero' cars in perfect condition for close-up shots and four for stunt driving and to carry the usual Bond gadgetry. Workshop supervisor Andy Smith was responsible for building the stunt cars. Both the Astons and the Jags had their engines and front suspension stripped out and replaced with a 300bhp Ford Boss 302 V8 and the four-wheel drive front end from a Ford Explorer. The extra traction was required for the chase scene filmed on the vast Jokulsarlon frozen lagoon in Iceland by George and Pierce Brosnan's stunt double Ray de Haan, which ends with the scene we saw being recorded on the set in Pinewood. Andy likes the Ford engine because

it is simple to work on but crucially very compact, and can be mounted at the back of the engine bay to improve weight distribution. He doesn't bother much with exhausts, which explains why the Vanquish we watched at Chobham sounded more NASCAR than supercar. Turns out that Andy himself lunched the Jaguar, shortly after giving his drivers a stern briefing on the importance of preserving the cars, though I doubt he noticed the extra deductions from his £1.5 million budget.

The engine also liberates space under the bonnet for special effects supervisor Chris Corbould's weaponry. A pair of machine guns made from machined aluminium emerge from under the Aston's bonnet vents, moving with incredible slickness and precision, and the front intake splits to reveal a row of rockets and another pair of machine guns; everything is operated by compressed air and controlled by a handheld panel of switches. All this is to counter Zao's rotary-barrelled machine gun and door-mounted heat-seeking missiles; you can guess who wins.

After following Bond's motorised exploits for so long, it was only right that we get to drive his car. The task fell to *Autocar*'s used car guru Chas Hallett; the venue was the Millbrook test track in Bedfordshire. He might be more Arthur Daley than

BELOW It's wise to move over if you see this in your rear-view mirror; fitting rockets to an XKR; workshop supervisor Andy Smith peers into the weapons bay, sorry, engine bay.

James Bond now, but as a former road tester he's well used to handling powerful cars, though not with the sort of firepower 007's Vanquish musters. The dash and steering wheel are much like a standard Vanquish, but there's a full roll cage and a row of toggle switches where the central console would be, controlling the car's rewired electrics. The Vanquish also loses its fancy sequential manual gearbox for a simple clutch and lever, the latter sprouting crudely from the floor.

The car starts with a ferocious roar, and despite being limited to a rather unheroic 40mph Chas returned praising its ride and the engine's flexibility, but cursing his inability to find the switches for the rockets. Perhaps he had visions of shooting up unscrupulous second-hand car dealers. It could be the plot for Bond's twenty-first adventure, where he goes in search of his latest nemesis, a bloke in a sheepskin coat, known only as Dave, who sold him a Maestro that turned out to be mostly filler. Halle Berry could be the beautiful trading standards officer determined to help him get his 500 quid back. We've suggested it, but Pierce isn't returning our calls. Maybe after the premiere...

ABOVE This may look like Pinewood Studios, but it's Iceland, actually. No really, it is.

LEFT Brosnan's stunt double, Ray de Haan; below, George Cottle takes Zao's Jag for a spin in the 'Icelandic ice palace' – aka Pinewood Studios.

END OF THE ROAD

DB7 GT Settling down into retirement? Not a chance. Meet the 435bhp GT, the most awesome Aston DB7 of all. *By Gavin Conway*

After nearly 10 years in our midst, a first sighting still takes your breath away. The Aston Martin DB7 sits below us in the parking lot while photographer Mark, an Aston Martin DB7 novice, packs away neat green boxes of 35mm film. A little distracted because he's thinking of 20 different things at once – that's the way these guys are – Mark wanders over with the clear signs of a query forming on his face.

He only gets as far as the window. Whatever thought he had has been permanently wiped away by the sight of the Aston and replaced with open-mouthed, gawping enthusiasm. This car has that effect, the power to take you out of yourself for a moment – a DB7 is an event in search of an audience.

It's very late in life for the DB7, though, and I suspect this might be my last coming together with designer Ian Callum's fabulous creation, with a hopefully less dramatic outcome than the first. In fact, this might be the last iteration of the DB7 that ever turns a wheel.

Launched in 1993, it has been the most successful Aston of all time. It started life with a 335bhp supercharged straight-six which was eventually replaced with a monumental 420bhp V12. When *Autocar* first drove the new and improved V12 DB back in '99, the verdict reflected just how far the car had come. It simply read: "double the cylinders, twice the car".

And yet it wasn't quite there, wasn't quite the full 10-star *Autocar* superstar that it could have been. The steering was slightly unresponsive, the gearshift a little long in the throw, the mid-range punch just this side of sensational.

And the Aston never seemed quite as serious as rivals such as the 911 about delivering the purest, most uncompromised, butt-tingling drive that money could buy. A bit like a slightly older tennis pro: a little more tanned than he should be, a little more likely to check his reflection in the shop window, a little less bothered about returning a centre-line power serve.

But something happens to sports pros when they see the end of the line coming: they always want one more shot at greatness before the long slide towards, well, Eastbourne, and a nice view from an over-heated apartment complex on the front.

That's why boxers always have one more fight than they really should. But then, who knows, maybe Tyson really will be champ again.

So meet the DB7 GT. Externally, this car needs about as much restorative surgery as Juliette Binoche: therefore the only clues to its new-found GT-ness are a couple of swollen, mesh-covered vents on the bonnet, new five-spoke 18-inch alloys, a mesh grille and a neat little integrated duck-tail spoiler on the bootlid.

Things get more serious on the dynamic front. The GT's engine has been remapped to deliver 435bhp, and there's been a corresponding increase in torque from 400 to 410lb ft. Those numbers aren't huge jumps, but the promise is much greater when combined with the new, lower final drive ratio. Aston has also equipped the GT with a racing twin-plate clutch and a shorter-throw shift action. To rein it all in, there are uprated brake boosters and radial grooved Brembo discs with pads designed to resist fade even after serious punishment.

The ride height has been lowered slightly and the suspension bushings stiffened up, along with revised

QUICK FACTS

Model	Aston Martin DB7 GT
Price	£104,500
On sale	February 2003
0–60mph	Under 5.0sec
Top speed	185mph (claimed)
Economy	14.2mpg
Emissions	476g/km CO_2

FEATURE

26 FEBRUARY 2003

Volume 235

No 9 | 5525

AUTOCAR
Special issue
26 February 2003 £2.10

20 EXTRA PAGES

F1 SEASON PREVIEW
YOUR GUIDE TO F1 IN 2003

WORLD EXCLUSIVE
ROVER'S NEW FOCUS RIVAL

FIRST DRIVES

NEW ROLLS
Does all-new Phantom mean Rolls now rocks?

NEW JAG
Brilliant new XJ: 'as good as an S-class'

Ford's £12k sex-bomb
STREETKA FIRST TEST

SPECIFICATIONS DB7 GT

ECONOMY

Urban	9.2mpg
Extra urban	20.7mpg
Combined	14.2mpg

DIMENSIONS

Length	4666mm
Width (inc mirrors)	2036mm
Height	1238mm
Wheelbase	2591mm
Weight	1622kg
Fuel tank	88 litres

ENGINE

Layout	12 cyls in vee, 5935cc
Max power	435bhp at 6000rpm
Max torque	410lb ft at 5000rpm
Power to weight	268bhp per tonne
Installation	Front, longitudinal, rwd
Made of	Aluminium alloy head and block
Valve gear	4 per cyl, dohc per bank
Ignition and fuel	Electronic ignition, sequential fuel injection

All figures are manufacturer's claims

GEARBOX

Type 6-speed manual by Tremec

SUSPENSION

Front Double wishbones, coil springs, dampers, anti-roll bar
Rear Double wishbones, coil springs, dampers, anti-roll bar

STEERING

Type Rack and pinion, power assisted
Turns lock-to-lock 2.7 turns

BRAKES

Front 355mm ventilated discs
Rear 330mm ventilated discs

WHEELS AND TYRES

Size 8Jx18in (f), 9Jx18 (r)
Made of Alloy
Tyres 245/40 ZR18 (f) 265/35 ZR18 (r)

THE **AUTOCAR** VERDICT

Now a better driver's car, with greater handling and performance. V12 is still one of the world's most impressive engines.

ABOVE RIGHT Cabin beautiful but a little too cramped; all-new five-spoke 18in alloys.

OPPOSITE GT's few exterior tweaks include bonnet vents and a mesh grille.

damper settings and stiffer steering rack mountings for better feedback. And Aston had help from John Miles, handling genius and ex-F1 pilot, in sorting the fine detail of the GT's down-the-road attitude.

So this is much more than a quick shot of vitamin B and a splash of Grecian 2000. This is Aston taking one more carefully aimed crack at the Porsche 911, which now looks, ironically, more like a DB7 than ever, especially around its greenhouse.

Starting up a DB7 is still a huge occasion. Ignition on, left hand hovering over the red start button. Punch it and the starter motor whirrs so fast that it sounds like an airgun at full chat. And then a not-so-neatly contained explosion and a mellow rumble from deep below – at start up, the engine is programmed to swing the revs right up to 2600rpm before settling to about 600. Before you've moved an inch, the Aston has delivered a fine piece of supercar theatre.

The gearchange is the first thing you'll notice. It's

brilliant: mechanical so that you can feel metal-on-metal, but fluid and oiled in its action with a short-throw providing the finishing touch.

So we unleash the V12 for a bit of a run. First thing is the noise, which is better than Ferrari-good thanks to an exhaust tuned more for your heart than for a quiet life. I find it nearly impossible not to downshift every few seconds; not just because the resultant rush to the 7000rpm limiter sounds like every great movie-chase soundtrack edited to one sensational seven-second riff, but because the six-speed manual gearbox is just so damn good to use.

Mid-range punch is also quite sensational. And with the traction control turned off – you will, you just know you will – you can slide the tail out in easily controllable drifts.

And this really does feel like a smaller DB7. The suspension changes make it more willing to change direction, and the car seems even less likely to

understeer. On a couple of clear-sighted slower corners where I anticipated understeer, it just didn't happen. And the telepathy of grip through the steering is so much better than I remember.

Then there is the Aston's interior environment. It's too small a cabin, no question, but the tangy aroma of the leather, the Alcantara overhead, that great-to-hold aluminium gearknob and the view over the rolling hills of bonnet make it an experience that gets far closer to the 10-star rating than the original V12 ever did. The only thing that'll make you wince is the creaking of the leather when you encounter rough roads. And the cramped driving position, which they'll solve only when an all new shell is created: enter next summer's DB9.

No question, the GT is the DB7's Rumble in the Jungle, one last convincing stab at greatness before the faded seaside and a quiet life beckon. But hell's bells, it's enough to make you believe growing old will be okay when it finally does happen.

ASTON: THE NEXT GENERATION

While the DB7 enjoys its last hurrah, pace is gathering on its replacement – the DB9. It's due next year, with power still provided by the Cosworth-designed 5.9-litre V12 packing around 440bhp – up 20bhp on the DB7.

The DB9 is based on an all-new aluminium chassis that will also provide the underpinnings for the 911-chasing DB8 in early 2005. A stiffer body structure and new suspension should bring ride and handling more up-to-date than today's Jaguar XK8-based model's set-up.

The power increase combined with a weight reduction benefit of using aluminium should push the 0-60 time below five seconds; currently it's 5.2sec. Top speed should be up slightly at around 190mph. While prices should stay around the DB7's £95k, a paddleshift 'box will be available for the first time, and a bespoke interior is also new.

Aston design boss Henrik Fisker is the man tasked with ensuring Aston's traditional design cues are maintained. The car is due to be unveiled at September's Frankfurt Motor Show.

Paul Barker

BOND IS BACK

`DB9` ...or at least he will be the minute he catches a glimpse of the stunning DB9. And with advanced construction and a shift-by-wire six-speed auto it ought to keep Q happy, too. *By Richard Bremner*

During the struggle for survival that has characterised much of Aston Martin's life, the company has had to battle even to introduce one significantly new model, let alone the three that it is readying for production over the next few years. Ford ownership and funding has been the great enabler here, but the Blue Oval is far from profligate with its cash, Aston boss Ulrich Bez working to a business plan that requires Aston's core models to be sired from the same platform if he is to realise his ambition of a range with three main models. That makes the first of these, the DB9 that you see here, important enough, but when you couple that with the fact that it is replacing the fastest-selling Aston Martin of all time, you begin to understand why Bez considers "a replacement for the DB7 is the company, the replacement of the company. It is that important".

The DB9, which goes on sale in April, will be followed by the V8 Vantage, which reaches showrooms early in 2005. The third model is the replacement for the Vanquish, though that will not appear for several years. The current Vanquish, you may recall, pioneered some of the body construction techniques employed on the DB9, but does not share its platform.

That the DB9 benefits from an all-new core structure, one idealised for Aston's purposes, is no small matter. A new platform is rare hardware in Aston history – the outgoing DB7 was based on the Jaguar XJS/XJ6 and, if the Virage was all-new structurally, the V8 preceding it was a development of the superleggera DB6/5/4 family. Never has Aston Martin had such resources behind it. But that didn't mean the company was free to develop multiple platforms, which was one reason why Bez canned the mid-engined car that had been under development when he arrived in July 2000.

As Dave King, the DB9's chief programme engineer,

explains: 'To get three models, we had to have one platform. We did concept studies into alternatives, but this was the most investment-efficient. A bonded and extruded frame is clearly the best. It offers good structural performance and allows Aston to be unique.' It's ideal for production runs of under 10,000, extrusions being cheap to tool for, even though their unit cost is high. The team's experience with the Vanquish 'gave us a lot of confidence,' says King.

How different the three cars will be to drive remains to be seen – as you can see from the pictures, it's not difficult to confuse their identities – but as we shall also see, Aston believes that with an assortment of differences affecting the powertrains, weight, dimensions, suspension and more, there will be a big difference in the driving characteristics of the DB9, the V8 Vantage and eventually, the new Vanquish.

Still, there's a good chance that a 2005 Vantage will feel familiar if you've driven a DB9, because front-seat occupants sit in the same position relative to a bulkhead and windscreen that will be the same in all three cars. That saves millions in development costs, not least crash engineering, as does shared packaging for the pedal box, steering column and air conditioning. The platform is also engineered to take two engines – a V12 and a V8 – a development King describes as 'a breakthrough'. The main difference between the DB9 and the V8 Vantage, he says, is in the wheelbase and the powertrains. 'And because the volumes are higher compared to the Vanquish we could invest more – so we have cast nodes and a formed backbone rather than a flat-panelled tunnel.' The result of which is rigidity 'significantly better than a Porsche Boxster's', though that car is open, of course. The DB9's crash performance 'was a big thing with our concept targets,' explains King. 'We've invested

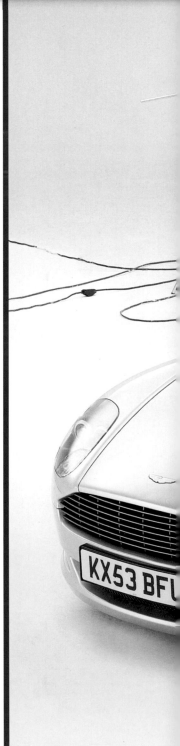

'A BONDED AND EXTRUDED FRAME OFFERS GOOD STRUCT-URAL PERFORMANCE AND ALLOWS ASTON TO BE UNIQUE'

our future in this, looking ahead about 10 years. That's about as far as you can go in crash legislation. We built rigs and rammed them into walls – with different gauges and sections sizes for the crash cans.

'Crash performance has been a huge step for us, and we've had a lot of help from Volvo – they've taken us under their wing.'

The DB9's transaxle rear suspension, 'was fundamental, because you've got the masses in the right place,' says King. 'A 50:50 weight distribution was prerequisite – this is the only way to do it.' Aston's engineers did a lot of benchmarking of Porsches, Ferraris, Maseratis, Jaguars and other products, he says: 'And then we set subjective targets. The old DB7 is an XJ6, with good noise suppression and low-speed ride. The DB9 is more direct, firmer-riding, but rounds off bumps. There's not as much isolation because we wanted more control.' The DB9's double-wishbone, coil-sprung suspension is shared with the V8 Vantage, but the more luxurious DB9 has double noise isolation at the rear, whereas the Vantage, with its single isolation barrier, trades refinement for the more precise rear-wheel control appropriate to its 911-challenging role. The Vantage's shorter wheelbase and 30kg weight-saving also makes a difference, as do different spring rates, damper settings, anti-roll bars, bushes and top-mounts. 'They're remarkably different in the way they drive,' King reckons. 'It's a tribute to our target-setting process.'

There are no trick electronic dampers for either DB9 or V8 Vantage and, while Aston considered electrically assisted power steering, says King, they decided that its tidy packaging offered no real benefits

DB9 weighs 1710kg, 140kg less than outgoing DB7, thanks to body frame claimed to be most structurally efficient in world considering its combination of strength, torsional rigidity and weight.

Innards here are Aston's VH platform, the basis for DB9, V8 Vantage and the next Vanquish. Frame and body 25 per cent lighter than DB7's, but doubly rigid. Platform a mix of diecast, stamped and extruded alloy, bonded using F1 and aircraft tech.

Compactly spaced double wishbone layout allows tips to lie within wheel diameter, enabling body to sit lower. Dampers fixed rate, no electro-trickery. Steering ZF hydraulic, bespoke, grooved brake discs.

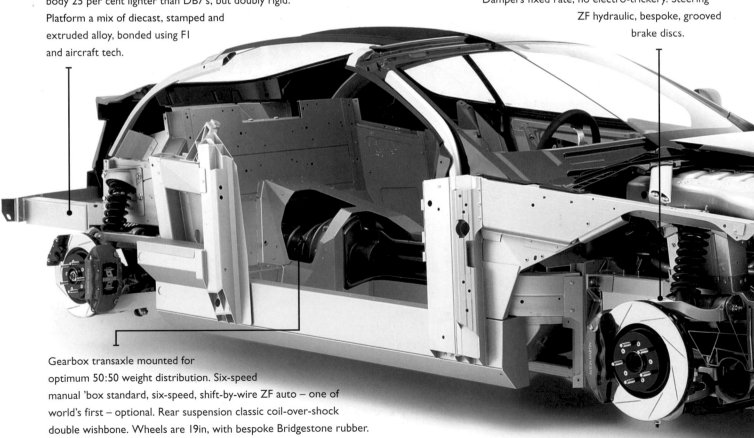

Gearbox transaxle mounted for optimum 50:50 weight distribution. Six-speed manual 'box standard, six-speed, shift-by-wire ZF auto – one of world's first – optional. Rear suspension classic coil-over-shock double wishbone. Wheels are 19in, with bespoke Bridgestone rubber.

DB7 V12 modified for 450bhp, more mid-range torque. Gets new crank, cams, manifolds, lube system, weighs 12kg less. Mounted well back for optimal weight distribution. Linked to 'box via solid torque tube.

Most exterior panels aluminium, glued in place by sole Aston robot, named James Bonder. Front wings and bootlid are composite, screen surround cast alloy – a first.

All crash testing carried out at Volvo facilities. Sacrificial crush cans allow for a 30mph accident without writing off the core structure. Dual-stage front airbags and sidebags are standard. Structure of platform eased process of tuning its crush characteristics.

SPECIFICATIONS DB9

Price	£103,000	Installation/management
On sale in UK	April 2004	Front, longitudinal, rear-wheel drive/
Top speed	186mph	Visteon engine management
0–60mph	4.7sec	**Transmission** 6-speed manual
MPG	na	**Steering** Rack and pinion, 3.0 turns
CO_2 emissions	na	**Suspension front/rear** Double
Engine	V12, 5935cc	wishbones, coil over dampers,
Power	450bhp at 6000rpm	anti-roll bar
Torque	420lb ft at 5000rpm	**Brakes front/rear**
Power to weight	263bhp per tonne	355/330mm ventilated discs
Compression ratio	10.3:1	**Tyres** 235/40 ZR19 (f), 275/35 ZR19 (r)

Driving position 'very special' – rearwards and very low, behind steep-raked screen. Ergonomics shared by all three VH cars, because bulkhead and screen are identical, saving development costs

Tidy centre console of automatic – it can self-shift or be operated via paddles. Park, reverse and neutral controlled by buttons – unusual. multiplex electrical architecture, developed with Volvo

Air conditioner and climate control, claimed to be among most compact and efficient in production, is used across all VH platform models, saving development time and cost

ABOVE Auto 'box gets paddles, too; dials and console shy away from Ford parts bin.

and that 'electric assistance has got a long way to go in terms of steering feel'. So the DB9 gets a hydraulic ZF rack with proportional assistance. 'It's all classic stuff, done well with good suppliers,' says King.

Under the bonnet is another classic – the familiar, for a lucky few, V12 as used in the Vanquish and DB7, tuned to deliver 450bhp rather than the outgoing DB7 GT's 435bhp. The DB9 has a better power-to-weight ratio than the Vanquish, which is 150kg heavier. Mid-range performance has also been beefed up, says King, courtesy of new cams, inlet and exhaust manifolds, a revised lubrication system and engine management system. The Vanquish, by contrast, offers more urge at the top end. Speaking of top end, there's no speed limiter, allowing a top speed of 186mph, though 189mph has been seen. The zero to 60mph sprint takes 4.7 seconds with the Graziano six-speed manual, while ZF's excellent six-speed automatic, which is also operable via paddles, needs 4.9 seconds. King reckons the manual 'box to have 'one of the best manual gearchanges in the world'.

An increasingly important signature for Aston is the exhaust note, given the Vanquish's magnificent aural emissions. King says a lot of time has been taken over this, the DB9 being a little more discreet than its

bigger brother. Ask him what he is proudest of, though, and he'll tell you: 'Weight: 1710kg is not light, but it's very good, 140kg less than the DB7 – and the V12 is not the lightest engine. Weight and efficiency are more important than power and brute force. We want to be known for making efficient cars.' He's also pleased with the package, 'which is no bigger than the car we're replacing', the DB9 being the same length, lower and a little wider, while providing a lot more cabin space.

What we have, then, is a car of advanced structure, ideal weight distribution, intelligent aerodynamics and competitive weight. Its conventional suspension allows for straightforward tuning and its potent, if slightly overweight, engine provides the necessary thrust. Being part of the Ford empire has enabled Aston to offer the DB9 with the best of contemporary sub-systems – which was just not possible in the old days – and a finely crafted cabin of traditional materials, inspired detail and modern design. And the logical thinking of the chief mind behind it – Ulrich Bez – shines as bright as the beauty of its shape. His team has created the most modern Aston ever.

Just how effective this combination turns out to be you can discover on 16 March, when *Autocar* publishes its world-exclusive first test of the DB9.

A FAMILY AFFAIR ASTON MARTIN DB9

Think the DB9 looks more than a little familiar? Well it's supposed to. Aston boss Ulrich Bez talks Julian Rendell through the family album

There is no mistaking the new DB9 is an Aston Martin – characteristic grille, sweeping roofline and powerful rear haunches. But these are design features that equally apply to its big and little brothers, the Vanquish and V8 Vantage. And, not surprisingly, critics mutter that the three cars look too similar, an impression reinforced by the public gaffes of Ford high-ups who, embarrassingly, have mistaken the three cars. For expensive, luxury items in which style is a key buying factor, it's potentially a serious shortcoming.

'I understand these comments totally,' says Aston Martin chief executive Uli Bez, 'and I have total sympathy with these people. But this is deliberate, we have to increase the visibility of Aston Martin by just having Aston Martins, not distinct models.'

In essence, Bez's view is that the styling of each of the three individual model lines must firstly be identified as an Aston Martin and secondly as a specific model. 'We do not want people to see an Aston Martin and a V8 Vantage. We just want people to see an Aston Martin,' he says.

His argument is that so few Aston Martins are on the road around the world that the brand is almost invisible, therefore the three models need an unambiguous family look to boost Aston Martin's brand image.

But won't that undermine each model's appeal with buyers? Why pay £165,000 for a Vanquish when a £70,000 V8 Vantage projects the same image? 'The important thing is that the owners know the difference, but they don't always want to show that off,' says Bez.

'We are selling the brand. And since we have shown the DB9, demand for the Vanquish is not down,' he adds.

Bez also reckons that other expensive luxury items, such as collector's watches, are not so easily distinguished by the casual observer. Significantly, he says watch enthusiasts know the subtleties: 'The difference is the expression of the design, the exclusivity and the prestige.'

And in such design details, Bez says the three Aston models are sufficiently different to have their own characters. At our exclusive picture shoot – the first time that even Bez had seen the three cars together – that was clear. But only after a forensic analysis of the design details.

The nuances of the V8 Vantage's short wheelbase, the Vanquish's pumped-up rear wheelarches and the DB9's elegant lines are just not obvious at first glance.

But Bez also believes that technology will distinguish the three Aston models by giving different driving characteristics, which will establish unique identities to smooth over the visual similarities: Vanquish as a flagship musclecar, DB9 as 2+2 GT and the V8 Vantage as a sporty two-seater. 'It's not just the hardware, it's the way we cook it together.'

To back up his argument, Bez draws on his experiences as a senior engineer at BMW and Porsche: 'The BMW 5-series is a very good car. Why do you need a 7-series? You sell it because it costs more and because it has a different character.

'And then look at the example of Porsche. There were people with a 911 and those with a 924. The 924 was never, never accepted as a true Porsche.'

Bez clearly doesn't want to make a similar mistake at Aston Martin: 'We need to nail the Aston Martin brand image and we will do that with our new model lines.'

VANQUISH Wide arches, square rear lamps and chrome trim distinguish flagship AM. Deep, wide grille flanked by circular fog lamps. Nose cone defines bonnet shut.

DB9 Smooth arches, flat boot deck and smaller diameter exhausts features of newest Aston. Headlamps rounder than Vanquish's; grille softer at edges. Foglamps next to intake.

V8 VANTAGE Baby coupé has smoked lenses, curvy boot deck and narrow hatch opening. Headlamps smaller. Grille like Vanquish's, but narrower. No foglamps.

DOUBLE-OH HEAVEN

VANQUISH To combat in-house competition from the DB9 and outside heat from Ferrari's 612, Aston has just given the Vanquish a lift. Andrew Frankel is the first journalist in the world to drive it

This morning dawned cold and clear. At 4.30am, I was walking out of a small Welsh cottage at the foot of the Brecon Beacons. In the half-light, I made my way across the drive to where the Vanquish waited.

At any time, in any place, an Aston Martin Vanquish is a thing to behold. But with the first rays of the new day glancing off the fine film of dew that had formed on its haunches, it had an almost ethereal beauty. I felt a spontaneous spasm of laughter burst out into the silent air. In that environment it was ridiculously, comically beautiful. And it was mine.

So, very early this morning, the Vanquish and I went and played. And six hours later I knew what you will learn in the next few minutes.

It had been a while. Three years ago I wrote *Autocar*'s road test on the car. I can remember how quickly it gained 175mph and how slowly it lost it again. The brakes were barely adequate. It hit 60mph in 4.4sec despite the need for a slow gearchange, but its handling was more grand tourer than sports car. It clung on well, but was as willing as Thatcher to change direction once its trajectory had been determined. Since then I've driven just two more, neither for long enough to be instructive.

This Vanquish is designed to address these issues. It doesn't look different, save for the nine-spoke alloys replacing the 12-spokers of the original, but beneath lies a car on which attention has been lavished in every area of its chassis' endeavour: springs, dampers, suspension layout, steering and brakes.

In the words of Aston CEO, Ulrich Bez, the changes are to make the Vanquish 'slightly sportier and more focused' and to that end it comes complete with stronger front uprights, shorter springs, firmer damping and a new front suspension wheel bearing assembly. The steering arms have been shortened,

speeding up the helm by 20 per cent, and the ride height dropped by 5mm.

Those new wheels reduce unsprung weight, but the real news is behind them: at the front the Brembo brake discs have been increased from 355mm to 378mm and have a 33 per cent greater thermal capacity in an attempt to eliminate the fade of the old system. The front calipers now have six instead of four pistons to give a 21 per cent increase in pad area. At the rear the discs retain their 330mm diameter but are 2mm thicker. Finally, Pagid competition pads are used. The original specification Vanquish remains, for a saving of £3000, but I suspect this is a similar strategy to that employed by leaving the six-cylinder DB7 in production after the introduction of the V12 Vantage. In practice, no one wanted one and it was quietly dropped.

None of this was obvious as I trickled out onto the road. The sound of its 460bhp, quad-cam, V12, 48-valve engine still moves you from the moment the first spark-plug fires and you find yourself warming it through gently, giving time for heat to build in the engine, gearbox and shock absorbers. It's silly, really, as the engine's heritage is linked to two conjoined Mondeo V6s, the gearbox's to a Chrysler Viper – but it's easy to expel such matters from your mind. I found myself thinking instead how much improved the Vanquish would be by oil temperature and pressure gauges. Enthusiasts like to know when their car is ready for exercise and a water temperature readout is worse than useless: it tells you the engine is warm when its oil remains stone cold.

By now the anticipation was almost palpable. The supercar game has changed over the years and it's something you have to understand before such a car can be enjoyed. Twenty years ago, supercars were the

'DROP YOUR ENTRY SPEED, GET THE CAR TURNED IN AND OPEN THE THROTTLE TO PUT THE CAR WHERE YOU NEED IT'

FIRST DRIVE

25 MAY 2004

Volume 240

No 8 | 5589

titans, the fastest things from one place to another via the medium of a twisting public road. But expect this £166,000 Aston Martin to cover such ground faster than certain £30,000 Mitsubishis and the outcome can only be a shattering disappointment. The importance of what these cars do diminishes daily, and in inverse proportion to the importance of the way in which they do it.

Then the time was right. Four tugs on the left-hand paddle and gearbox leapt seamlessly from a loping sixth to a screaming second. Throttles wide open, it sat back, gathered itself and speared forward. Listening to the noise, I almost convinced myself I could break down its components into every punch of a piston, whizz of a valve and sweep of the crankshaft, so multi-layered and well-defined is its note.

The gearchange comes swiftly and easily – someone's worked on the software since I was last here – and now we're getting into the Vanquish's world. Work the car in third and fourth gear and it comes alive like an old Ferrari Daytona does above 100mph. It feels unfettered from its 1800kg-plus weight through fast, sweeping curves, the grip of its Yokohamas a given, the precision of its steering

a delight. That trace of float has been exorcised by the new suspension; it's still no Jason Robinson when changing direction, but you shouldn't have to expect that from such a car: what matters is that the Vanquish now flows from fast bend to fast bend with authority and commitment, the steering as quick and communicative as you could hope to find in a heavy, front-engined car. In this environment, the revisions work just fine. But for their undoubted power, the new brakes are still not quite right. The fade has gone (the next day they coped with five laps of Goodwood, braking hard from 150mph at the end of the straight), but the feel is not there. I found myself thinking about them as each corner approached, the sure sign that all is not as it should be. Instead of taking instinctive stabs at the left pedal, I had to consider what load to apply and then modify it accordingly as the speed washed away.

And as curving country lanes gave way to uncompromising mountain roads, more limitations became apparent. For all its grip, this is not a car to aim into a corner too fast and hope to sort it out on the way through; do that and you will run wide, and you'll need to take care shutting the throttle to bring the car back on line. It's much better to adopt the old-

fashioned approach and drop your entry speed, get the car turned in and then open the throttle to put the car where you need it. Do this and the rewards rain down, all the way from the perfect line through the bend to the readily available powerslide at the exit. It seems odd to use the phrase 'old fashioned' in the context of the Vanquish, launched just three years ago as, by Aston standards, a technological miracle. Yet that's how it feels. Its driving position is strange: the wheel is too far away, the switchgear is a mess and you can see very little out of the back.

It is entirely deliberate that I have waited this long before mentioning 'DB9', but it cannot be ignored. Who, after all, would pay an extra £62,000 for a Vanquish when a DB9 has better handling, a more comfortable ride and a superior power-to-weight ratio? By any objective assessment, the Vanquish goose has been well and truly cooked by its celebrity chef sister.

But I can still – just – see its point. Have no doubt that the DB9 would be the better car at the same price, but the Vanquish still has a charm of its own. If heritage is important, this is the last car Newport Pagnell will build. If handcraftsmanship is your thing, its aluminium panels are still hit by men with hammers. And if you're after exclusivity, remember that for every eight DB9s that roll off the shiny new line at Gaydon, just one Vanquish will be assembled in Newport Pagnell.

And then there are the looks. At first I preferred the DB9, but now I find the Vanquish shape more arresting, its squat stance drawing my gaze more than the prettier, less pugnacious DB9.

It adds up to one key strength it holds over its astonishing stablemate, a characteristic best described by example. Give me a DB9 or a Vanquish to drive and I'd choose the younger car every time until someone told me I'd never drive another Aston again. Then, for one last blast, I'd take the Vanquish. Its technical inferiority would be of no consequence then: its job would be to leave an imprint of Aston Martin on my brain, one which would conjure both the strengths and the weaknesses without which no memory of this most enigmatic marque could be fully formed.

You can say the Vanquish has the greater sense of occasion or that the DB9 is too bloody good; I choose merely to celebrate the fact that their paths have overlapped. Though a more powerful Vanquish is on the way, one day too soon it will be gone. It is the bridge between Aston's extraordinary past and undoubtedly glorious future, and we will never see its like again.

SPECIFICATIONS VANQUISH

Price	£166,000	**Installation** Front, longitudinal,	
On sale in UK	May 2004	rear-wheel drive	
Top speed	196mph	**Transmission** 6-speed manual	
0–60mph	4.4sec	with Automatic Shift Manual	
0–100mph	10.5sec	**Suspension front/rear** Double	
MPG	16.9	wishbones, anti-roll bars, coil springs	
Insurance group	20	**Brakes** 378mm (f), 330mm (r)	
Engine	V12, 5925cc	ventilated discs	
Power	460bhp at 6500rpm	**Tyres** Alloy, 255/40 ZR19 (f),	
Torque	400lb ft at 5000rpm	285/40 ZR19 (r), Yokohama	

ASTON MARTIN DB9

As the first true product of the new Aston Martin, and successor to the best-selling Aston ever, the DB9 has an awful lot to prove. And it is more than up to the job

Aston Martin couldn't have launched the DB9 in more competitive times if it had personally engineered the current coupé scenery. Ferrari sales are bouyant, Porsche is talking increased volumes, Lamborghini has emerged as a serious player and Bentley has a new two-door. If it wasn't already difficult enough to replace the DB7 – the most beautiful Aston in a generation and the most successful ever made – then those tantalising alternatives have heaped even more pressure on the company.

Behind the scenes, everything has changed at Aston. Conceptually, the £103,000 DB9 continues an engineering philosophy begun with the Vanquish, but in reality this is the first car to come out of the company's new Gaydon facility, and to fully benefit from all its resources.

DESIGN AND ENGINEERING ★★★★★
Intelligent transmission; beautiful to look at

Traffic jams will be commonplace around parked DB9s. The car is so gracefully beautiful, so instinctively Aston Martin, that people are forced to stop and stare. Identifying weak aspects of Henrik Fisker's design is virtually impossible, and that's a rare thing in this type of car. It's less muscular than a Vanquish, but

more consistent, particularly around the rear end. Shut-lines are millimetre-perfect and the headlight units suitably ornamental.

The aristocracy probably won't be overjoyed to learn that their sports car manufacturer of choice is now gluing its cars together. But that's the truth of the matter. Aston Martin has effectively taken the technology used by Lotus on the original Elise, honed it during three years of Vanquish production and now developed a modular application for this car, next year's V8 Vantage and potential future models.

The basic structure is bonded aluminium and has immense torsional and crash strength: it's twice as stiff as a DB7's, and 25 per cent lighter. The process itself is fascinating and potential owners can visit the factory to see an immense robot, aptly named James Bonder, applying adhesive to metal at incredible, laser-guided speed. From this impressive platform, Aston has allowed its chassis engineers to really go to town. Classic coil-over-shock double wishbones sit at each corner of the 2740mm wheelbase, with 19in wheels attached to the hubs. There's no electronic damper control and no electric power steering. Weight distribution and polar moment of inertia (PMI, effectively centre of mass) were an engineering obsession for the chassis team, and they are thrilled at having achieved a 50:50 front/rear weight split and a PMI ideally suited to the DB9's sporting GT credentials.

The drivetrain is similarly impressive. The 6.0-litre V12 is borrowed from the Vanquish and outgoing DB7 Vantage, but is thoroughly revised (new crank, camshafts, manifolds and oil system). Outputs are 450bhp at 6000rpm and an impressive 420lb ft at 5000rpm. Even though the engine speed at peak torque appears to indicate otherwise, the engine has been tuned for mid-range performance. But the transmission is the key to the DB9's multi-faceted appeal. Aston is the first manufacturer to offer a genuine sports-oriented, downshift-matching, paddle-shift gearbox based on an automatic, rather than a manual. The potential advantages are immense: a

QUICK FACTS

Model tested	Aston Martin DB9
List price	£103,000
Top speed	186mph
30–70mph	4.6sec
0–60mph	5.4sec
70–0mph	46.8m
Average test MPG	12.1
For	Brilliant transmission, looks and interior
Against	Heavy brakes and steering, tyre noise

ROAD TEST

1 JUNE 2004

Volume 240

No 9 I 5590

choice of immediate, finger-nudge shifts one minute or full access to the world's finest auto (the ZF six-speed) at the touch of a button the next.

PERFORMANCE/BRAKES ★★★★
Ample pace superbly delivered, brakes heavy

There's not much that will out-drag a DB9 in a straight line. Given the current German obsession with horsepower, that means the Aston has more than enough performance to satisfy its intended market. In fact, it has a surplus.

But just as the 6.0-litre V12 hasn't been tuned purely for maximum power, so the performance it offers and the way it allows the driver to access its considerable potential has been subtly managed. In short, there isn't a better drivetrain on sale. There are more powerful units and faster-changing gearboxes, but nothing that matches the DB9's desirability, sense of occasion and sheer usability.

Use the dash-mounted buttons to select Drive and the DB9 is a conventional automatic. One that with the ESP disengaged summons impressive traction for a front-engined/rear-drive coupé, and chirps its way to 30mph in 2.0sec. From the moment the exhaust valving acknowledges full throttle and bellows its first distinctive 12-pot blare, both shove and soundtrack remain consistently joyous all the way to 160mph. Then wind resistance begins to impede thrust, and velocity leaves the brass section behind too quickly for it to be heard in the cabin.

ABOVE Ride harsher than the DB7's, but excellent damping makes up for it; steering accurate but over-heavy.

LEFT Graceful styling looks great from any angle; even the handbook is beautiful; clever handles instinctive to use.

ROAD TEST DB9

MAXIMUM SPEEDS

6th	186mph/5110rpm	5th	186/6596
4th	149/6750	3rd	111/6750
2nd	72/6750	1st	41/6750

ACCELERATION FROM REST

True mph	seconds	speedo mph
30	2.0	30
40	2.9	41
50	4.4	51
60	5.4	62
70	6.6	73
80	8.1	83
90	9.6	92
100	11.3	104
110	13.5	113
120	15.9	124
130	18.6	133
140	22.2	143
150	26.9	152

Standing qtr mile 13.7sec/111mph
Standing km 24sec/146mph
30–70mph through gears 4.6sec
20–70mph in 4th 15.8sec

ACCELERATION IN GEAR

MPH	6th	5th	4th	3rd	2nd
20–40	–	–	–	2.8	2.1
30–50	–	–	4.1	3.0	2.0
40–60	7.7	6.1	4.2	3.1	1.9
50–70	8.1	6.1	4.1	3.0	2.1
60–80	8.3	6.1	4.2	2.8	–
70–90	8.7	6.1	4.2	2.9	–
80–100	9.2	6.5	4.1	3.2	–
90–110	9.8	6.8	4.2	3.9	–
100–120	10.8	7.0	4.4	–	–
110–130	–	7.4	5.2	–	–
120–140	–	–	6.0	–	–
130–150	–	–	–	–	–

FUEL CONSUMPTION

Average/best/worst/touring
12.1/15.7/8.5/15.7mpg

Urban/combined	11.3/17.1mpg
Tank capacity	85 litres
Theoretical range	320 miles
Real-world range	294 miles

BRAKES

30/50/70mph	7.5/24.6/46.8 metres
60–0mph	2.7sec

Pedal feel poor/fair/good/**excellent**
Fade poor/fair/good/**excellent**

HANDLING AND RIDE

Normal driving
Balance understeer/oversteer/**neutral**
Steering feel poor/fair/**good**/excellent
Body control poor/fair/good/**excellent**
Ride quality poor/**fair**/good/excellent
Grip poor/fair/good/**excellent**

Hard driving
Balance understeer/oversteer/**neutral**
Steering feel poor/fair/**good**/excellent
Body control poor/fair/good/**excellent**
Ride quality poor/fair/**good**/excellent
Grip poor/fair/good/**excellent**

Test notes Ride is always firm,
especially in town, but the trade-off is
genuine composure for a big GT when
driven hard. Grip levels high, although
the DB9 can be steered on the throttle.
A high kerb weight means too much of
this will take its toll on tyres.

NOISE

Idle/max revs in 3rd 57/85dbA
30/50/70mph 61/67/72dbA
Sound quality poor/fair/good/**excellent**

HEADLIGHTS

Dipped beam poor/fair/**good**/excellent
Full beam poor/fair/good/**excellent**
Test notes Excellent clarity and
spread of light, especially on full beam.

TESTER'S NOTES

The owner's manual says that the car's
computer records all manner of data,
and that in the event of an accident that
data can be released to the relevant
authorities. Best take a lawyer down to
the showroom before signing on the line.

Remembering its GT pretensions, the fact no
gearlever has needed stirring, and no powershifts
executed to trim tenths of a second, the DB9's
acceleration figures are pretty impressive: rest to
60mph in 5.4sec, rest to 100mph in 11.3sec and rest
to 150mph in 26.9sec. Slightly slower than the first car
we figured in France, true, but still decently competitive
within the price structure in this class.

And when there's the need to have more control
over shift points and gear selection, just nudge one
of the paddles for the manual override. No, it can't
change quite as swiftly as the best hydraulically actuated
manual 'boxes, but it's so much closer to their speed
than they are to matching its smoothness in auto mode
that this gearbox automatically renders everything, bar
Audi's DSG system, obsolete. Upshifts are crisp and
brisk, and coming down the 'box has the ECU insert a
perfect heel 'n' toe blip to smooth the change.

Braking performance is very good, helped no doubt

SPECIFICATIONS DB9

DIMENSIONS

Min/max front legroom 915/1095mm Min/max front headroom 875/925mm
Min/max rear legroom 380/560mm Rear headroom 755mm Kerb weight 1760kg
Min/max boot width 665/1515mm Boot height 460mm Boot volume 172 litres/dm³
Front/rear tracks 1568/1562mm Width (with/without mirrors) 2017/1875mm

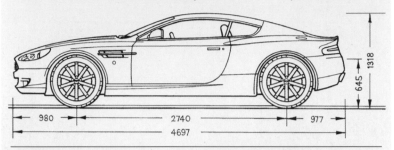

1318
645
980 2740 977
4697

ENGINE

Layout	V12, 5935cc
Power	450bhp at 6000rpm
Torque	420lb ft at 5000rpm
Max engine speed	6750rpm
Specific output	76bhp per litre
Power to weight	256bhp per tonne
Torque to weight	239lb ft per tonne
Installation	Longitudinal, front, rear-wheel drive
Construction	Alloy heads & block
Bore/stroke	89.0/79.5mm
Valve gear	4 per cyl, dohc
Compression ratio	10.3:1
Management	Visteon

TRANSMISSION

Gearbox 6-speed automatic

Ratios/mph per 1000rpm

Final drive ratio 3.15:1

1st 4.17/6.0		2nd 2.34/10.7	
3rd 1.52/16.5		4th 1.14/22.0	
5th 0.89/28.2		6th 0.69/36.4	

CHASSIS AND BODY

Body	Two-door coupé, Cd 0.34
Wheels	Alloy 8.0J x 19in (f), 9.0J x 19in (r)
Tyres	235/40 ZR19 (f), 275/35 ZR19 (r)
	Bridgestone Potenza RE050
Safety	Driver, passenger and side airbags, seatbelt pretensioners, DSC (Dynamic Stability Control), traction control

STEERING

Type	Rack and pinion, power assistance
Turns lock-to-lock	3.0
Turning circle	11.5m

SUSPENSION

Front Double wishbones, coil springs, anti-roll bar

Rear Double wishbones, coil springs, anti-roll bar

BRAKES

Front 355mm ventilated discs

Rear 330mm ventilated discs

Anti-lock Standard, with brake assist and brakeforce distribution

THE SMALL PRINT © *Autocar* 2004. For further information on the Aston Martin DB9 contact Aston Martin, Banbury Road, Gaydon, Warwick CV35 0DB (01908 610620), www.astonmartin.co.uk. The cost-per-mile figure is calculated over three years/ 36,000 miles and includes depreciation, maintenance, road tax, funding and fuel, but not insurance. Figure supplied by Lloyds TSB Autolease (0870 600 6333). The insurance quote is for a 35-year-old professional male with a clean licence and full no-claims bonus, living in Swindon, supplied by What Car? Insurance. Contract hire figure is based on a lease for three years/36,000 miles, includes maintenance and is supplied by Lombard (0870 902 3311).

---

by the excellent (for a big GT) 1710kg kerb weight. The big grooved discs only begin to show fade after 10 consecutive 100mph stops, but the pedal feel doesn't match the performance. It requires a concerted push even from moderate speed; the effort levels are simply too high.

HANDLING AND RIDE ★★★★
Fine compromise exposed on poor surfaces

There are compromises in the DB9's chassis that some UK owners will find annoying, but even so, it remains a fine blend of comfort and agility.

By conventional Aston standards, the DB9 is very firmly sprung – much stiffer than the car it replaces – so it's quite natural that the car transmits copious surface information into the cabin. There's more sound-deadening than in the Vanquish, but over a pitted B-road or poor A-road the DB9 jiggles the way every 190mph sports car does. Double wishbones and 19in Bridgestone rubber were always going to struggle to facilitate a genuinely supple ride, but the Aston compensates with beautifully controlled damping regardless of speed. Yes, you are deflected by surprisingly small intrusions, but they're always sorted in one movement.

This, coupled with a very accurate steering rack, lends the DB9 an agility well beyond its size. It can't be threaded with 911-confidence when the hedgerows close in and the roads get narrow, but then it doesn't intimidate either.

The limited-slip differential is tight, though. Tight enough for sideways heroics on minimal throttle in the wet, with the ESP disengaged. On a dry surface only the insane will try to find where the grip finally ends: the car is supremely neutral with a deliberate dose of understeer, which then gives way to oversteer in the most extreme cases.

Steering feel is always going to take a hit in something this big and hydraulically assisted: the DB9 offers a reasonable flow of information, but the weighting is curiously heavy. Heavy enough to induce a (false) feeling of inertia in the steering apparatus that makes directing the DB9 feel harder than it really is. It's an odd choice, given how hard the engineers have worked on the chassis' physical ability to change direction.

Surface sensitivity and wind noise are the other problems. On our multi-lane roads the DB9 struggles to suppress tyre noise from its 235-section front and 275-section rear tyres, and there's noticeable A-pillar ruffle above 80mph, to the extent that it operates on the outer limits of GT-style comfort.

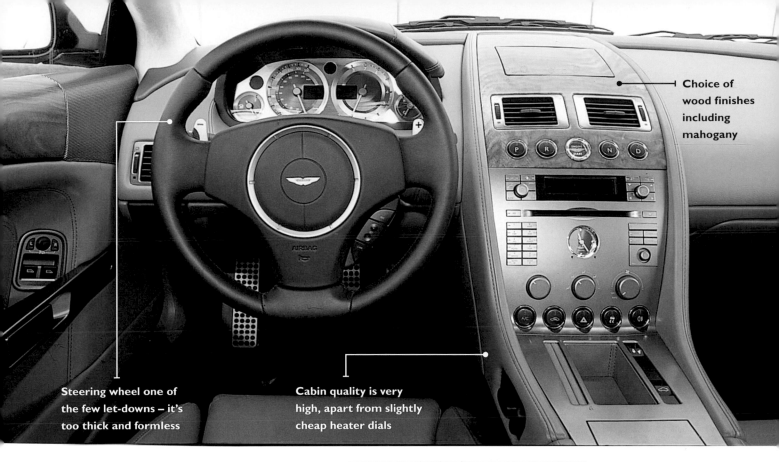

Choice of wood finishes including mahogany

Steering wheel one of the few let-downs – it's too thick and formless

Cabin quality is very high, apart from slightly cheap heater dials

ABOVE Top quality materials help make cabin feel special; driving position good, but scuttle limits visibility.

LEFT Sat-nav screen rises from dash; boot holds a reasonable 172 litres.

SAFETY AND EQUIPMENT ★★★★
Wonderful for two, and immensely strong

Central to Aston's three-tier range is the notion of the DB9 being a two-plus-two and therefore not competing with big-brother Vanquish. Fair enough, the car does have a pair of beautifully trimmed rear seats, but even if Ronnie Corbett and Kylie Minogue decided to have little ones, they would struggle to use them. In fact, anyone over four-and-a-half feet tall would. The DB9 isn't a two-plus-two, and it isn't even a two-plus-one-to-the-pub-and-back. It's a two-seater with lovingly trimmed luggage cubbies behind the sumptuously cow-covered Recaros.

But what a cabin. As a visual and tactile interpretation of what a combination of traditional

WHAT IT COSTS

ASTON MARTIN DB9

On-the-road price	£103,000
Price as tested	£107,920
CO₂	349g/km
Tax at 22/40% pcm	£513/933
Cost per mile	na
Contract hire/month	na

INSURANCE

Insurance/typical quote	20/£2501

WARRANTY

36 months/unlimited miles

EQUIPMENT CHECKLIST

Sat-nav	**£1750**
Parking sensors	**£295**
Heated front seats	**£295**
Heated screen	**£295**
Mid-spec Linn hi-fi	**£1495**
Cruise control	**£295**
Mahogany wood	**£495**
Airbag driver/passenger/side	■/■/■
GSM phone	£795

Options in **bold** fitted to test car
■ = Standard na = not available

THE CLASS

ASTON MARTIN DB9 £103,000 ★★★★⯪

Capacity 5935cc
Power 450bhp
Torque 420lb ft
0–60mph 5.4sec
Max speed 186mph
CO_2 349g/km

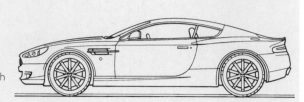

Forget complaints about derivative styling – the DB9 is stunning. We'd prefer a lighter helm and a slightly more composed ride, but the perfect match of V12 and auto 'box more than makes amends. Good value.

FERRARI 612 SCAGLIETTI £170,500 ★★★★

Capacity 5748cc
Power 540bhp
Torque 434lb ft
0–60mph 4.2sec
Max speed 196mph
CO_2 475g/km

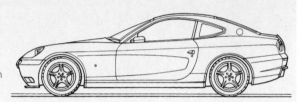

An outstanding car from Ferrari. Manages to blend real pace – both in a straight line and around corners – with genuine four-seat practicality and comfort. If only it didn't look the way it does. A missed opportunity.

MERCEDES-BENZ CL65 £120,000   first drive 2.9.03

Capacity 5980cc
Power 603bhp
Torque 738lb ft
0–60mph 4.4sec
Max speed 155mph
CO_2 357g/km

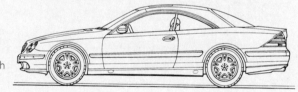

With the sort of power and torque outputs produced by the mighty CL65, it's not surprising that derestricted, it's the fastest four-seater in the world. All it needs is a higher-quality cabin and a prestigious badge.

PORSCHE 911 TURBO £88,240 ★★★★★

Capacity 3600cc
Power 420bhp
Torque 413lb ft
0–60mph 3.9sec
Max speed 189mph
CO_2 309g/km

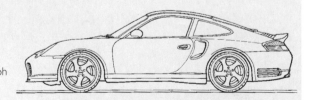

As usual, the 911 goes its own way and in doing so will either appeal massively or not even register as a rival. Stunning reserves of power, grip, handling and braking, but rear seats marginal for adults.

and contemporary Aston detailing should look like, it's a triumph. Yes, the rotary heater controls feel cheap and the headlamp switch is nasty, but the rest is a joy.

From the multi-adjustable electric seat you face an instrument binnacle of unrivalled flamboyance in the car world. Its silver faces and three-dimensional aspect make it difficult to read in some lights, but it looks wonderful. The computer read-outs are all finely pixellated and glow a sultry green. A Linn hi-fi sits in the centre console, with a six-disc changer, and the sat-nav display is cleverly recessed into the slab of wood on the dash-top.

Trim quality is beyond question. The hides look, feel and smell expensive. The clever use of different woods such as mahogany and bamboo (not mixed together but both available as options) works brilliantly. The only ergonomic gripes are a poorly shaped steering wheel (too thick, too formless) and a slightly intimidating driving position: it's a long old nose and not being able to see over the scuttle can be a problem.

This new breed of Astons need long lifecycles, so the DB9 has been built to comply with all foreseeable crash legislation. The company is fiercely independent, and is keen to point out it hasn't relied on other PAG group members for any components,

but is happy to admit that Volvo was immensely helpful in this process. Its Swedish facility was used to create a vehicle capable of sustaining a 30mph head-on without needing core structural repairs, and a cabin with dual-stage front and side airbags as standard. Given how pedestrian-friendly its bonnet is, a fine NCAP result seems likely.

RUNNING COSTS ★★★★
Best residuals in the UK

We're always cautious when pairing the word value with a car whose sticker price belongs in the window of an estate agent, but there's no getting round the fact that the DB9 is a steal. It's more desirable than a Ferrari 612 Scaglietti and yet it costs £67,000 less. That's absurd. It has so much more image and style than the £99,069 Porsche 911 Turbo with optional Power Kit that the comparison seems unfair. And with a waiting list stretching into 2007 already, residuals are looking very strong.

Running the DB9 won't be cheap. Our overall average fuel consumption was 12.1mpg (although a figure in the high teens is possible), slipping to 8.5mpg at the track. This makes the 85-litre tank merely adequate. The 349g/km CO_2 figure puts it into the top company car tax band.

LEFT Top quality materials help make cabin feel special; flamboyant dials look gorgeous.

BELOW LEFT Graceful styling looks great from any angle.

AUTOCAR VERDICT

Dealing with the bad is a gratifyingly short process with the DB9. Its steering is too heavy, as is the brake pedal, the ride is choppy on poor surfaces and a few of the switches are unbecoming of a £103k car. Other than that, as you have probably guessed, we are consumed with admiration for what Aston has achieved with this car. It has a near-perfect transmission connected to a musical instrument of a V12 that together provide ideal performance in both quantity and quality of delivery. More gratifying still is just how well the team that created it understand what they want Aston to be, and how closely those aspirations fit with customer demands.

And yet, for all the dynamic achievements, much of the DB9's success must be attributed to its looks. There are very few genuinely beautiful cars replete with full 360-degree walk-round perfection, but this is one such car. People cannot believe how graceful it is in the flesh: they just point and stare. That, even more than a delightful cabin and polished dynamics, is the real denominator of success. It matches the emotive appeal of a Ferrari or Lamborghini, adds its own brand of practicality and offers a driving experience unmatched for its versatility and all-round appeal. Extraordinarily desirable and supremely capable, the DB9 is the best car Aston Martin has ever made and a tantalising preview of what's to come from Gaydon.

Stunning British GT

V-MAX

VANQUISH S The 200mph Vanquish S isn't just the fastest-ever Aston Martin, it's the car the Vanquish always should have been. *By Chris Harris*

Today I'm thinking strange thoughts. One keeps coming back as I carefully nose the fastest Aston Martin ever made around Bristol. Would Isambard Kingdom Brunel have been happy with the sport shift mapping on the new £174,000 Vanquish S? Brunel died before the technology that would have such a profound effect on human lives – the internal combustion engine – had been invented, but the answer would still have been a definite 'no'. Were he alive, IKB would reckon it too slow and too harsh as the hydraulically actuated clutch re-meshes the cogs. Then he'd set about fixing it.

As a visitor, it's difficult to walk anywhere in Bristol and not be reminded of the influence he had over its major architecture and his notable engineering successes. But as a Bristolian the bond is stronger. Not through pride, though: Bristolians are too pragmatic for that. A local taxi driver summed it up perfectly for me a few years ago: 'Well, we'd be stuffed without our Kingdom. No train station for gettin' 'em 'ere, no boat for lookin' at and no bridge for walkin' over.'

So we're going to saunter around his train station (Temple Meads), his boat (the SS *Great Britain*) and his bridge (the Clifton Suspension Bridge) in Aston's revised Vanquish S. After the closure of Jaguar's Browns Lane plant I feel the need to celebrate some British engineering, current and past, though I'll stop short of sticking small plastic St George motifs on the side windows.

Tellingly, no one in Bristol has any idea that this is a significantly different car to a standard Vanquish. The only way of spotting it is the rather scrappy S motif on the bootlid which, along with a boot-lip spoiler, a redesigned front grille and a sizeable front splitter, add a dose of seriousness to the standard shape from most angles. Such subtleties are insignificant when the basic Aston shape can divert glances from a hundred yards.

We really feared for the Vanquish when we first drove a DB9 earlier this year. But despite

FIRST DRIVE

28 SEPTEMBER 2004

Volume 241

No 13 | 5607

the presence of an in-house infant phenomenon, Vanquish sales have remained strong; Aston will still make 350 this year. The situation is the same at Lamborghini – demand for the Murciélago is still remarkably high despite the new Gallardo – and it proves that people are graduating up from lesser brands and not trading down. It seems that in the world of big-number cars, those with the biggest wallets will always want the most expensive toys.

Beautiful though the DB9 might be, this car has twice the presence. Compound that with the fact that it makes twice the noise and somehow much of the staggering £71,000 price difference between DB9 and Vanquish S is justified. The Vanquish's case is made even stronger by what is bolted between the front suspension uprights. This is the engine the car should have had from the start: 520bhp sounds like the sort of poke one might expect from a 5.9-litre Aston V12.

Squeezing out the extra 60bhp over the standard Vanquish has been pretty hard work, though. The engine gets revised cylinder heads with reprofiled inlet ports and combustion chambers, stronger con rods, a higher compression ratio, new injectors and a remapped ECU to take advantage of the improved fuelling and airflow. For the same increase on a Porsche 911 Turbo, you just insert a screwdriver

into the boost controller and crank it in the direction marked schnell. But then this is about as far removed from Porsche's philosophy as it gets.

This, finally, is the definitive front-engined two-seat British super GT. The S doesn't correct all of the basic car's flaws, but it gets closer to the car Brunel might have built, and addresses enough of them to allow the Vanquish's considerable character to shine through undiminished. Until earlier this year, the Vanquish's main strengths against a Ferrari 575 Maranello's were its styling and engine noise. Then the 'Dynamics' pack was introduced, with uprated suspension, steering and brakes. It closed the gap significantly. This car takes those settings and adds its 520bhp at 7000rpm and 425lb ft at a high-ish 5800rpm to create a car that is finally a match for the Ferrari.

I'd be less happy rolling it around the Hotwells area to gain a shot of SS *Great Britain* if I hadn't had the chance to hammer the Aston across the Midlands earlier in the day. A combination of long bonnet, chunky A-pillar and considerable price make it scary enough to drive around town, but it's the control weights that add to the intimidation factor. The steering's heavy, as are the brake and throttle pedals. In fact, the Vanquish is rather corpulent – 1835kg at the kerb. Still, Brunel would have been fascinated by its bonded aluminium construction.

BELOW Aston has managed to bring extra control where the car desperately needed it, without having it crash across anything less than a croquet-lawn surface; subtle 'S' badge hints at extra 60bhp over regular Vanquish; mighty 5.9-litre V12 now produces 520bhp and 425lb ft, and it makes a noise to shame a Ferrari 575 Maranello.

And I still don't get on with those gearshift paddles. Around town you should use the automatic function, but either my throttle inputs aren't to the liking of the gearbox's brain or the changes are far too slow in response to a pushed pedal. The manual change is easier, but standard parking manoeuvres can put years on the driver. The clutch smells worse than an Intercity 125's brakes after an emergency stop. And this is a car that will spend as much time (if not more) stumbling around Mayfair as it will on moorland roads.

It's a shame there aren't more hyper-wealthy types in Clifton, because the Vanquish looks sharper parked in front of the suspension bridge than it does anywhere else in the UK. A liberal smattering of them in dark metallic shades would certainly aid the view, but then I'm biased. There's no point trying to cosy the car and bridge together in terms

of importance: even a Vanquish seems utterly inadequate in front of arguably the finest example of Victorian engineering.

The changes made to the Aston's chassis aren't revolutionary, but they are certainly effective. It sits 5mm lower than the standard car, has a 20 per cent quicker steering rack and firmer springs and dampers. It's certainly a little lumpier around town, but then the basic car's no limo. Aston has managed to bring extra control where the car desperately needed it without having it crash across anything less than a croquet-lawn surface. But it's a crime jerking the car around town, so we head out on the M4 to Wales and some very fast, empty roads.

The Vanquish isn't too bad on the motorway. That strange driving position remains (wheel too far away, seat too high) and tyre noise from the Yokohamas is pronounced – they like to report

ABOVE Vanquish S firmer but body control far superior than standard model's; heavy controls make town driving hard work.

'THE CHANGES ARE SUBTLE; THE CUMULATIVE EFFECT THEY REAP MORE SIGNIFICANT THAN I'D EXPECTED'

SPECIFICATIONS VANQUISH S

Price	£174,000	**Transmission**	6-speed manual	
On sale in UK	September 2004	with Automatic Shift Manual		
Top speed	200mph	**Suspension front/rear** Double		
0–60mph	4.8sec	wishbones, coil springs, anti-roll bar		
0–100mph	9.8sec	**Brakes front/rear**		
MPG	16.9	378mm/330mm ventilated discs		
Insurance group	20	**Tyres front/rear**		
Engine	V12, 5925cc	255/40 ZR19 / 285/40 ZR19		
Power	520bhp at 7000rpm	**Dimensions**		
Torque	425lb ft at 5800rpm	Length 4665mm	Width	1923mm
Power to weight	283bhp per tonne	Height 1318mm	Weight	1835kg
Installation	Front, longitudinal,	Wheelbase	2690mm	
	rear-wheel drive	Fuel tank	80 litres	

back the surface grade at all times. But the hi-fi's excellent and the new winged bucket seats are more supportive than the standard items. The view is also far more attractive because the grey plastic centre console is now covered in leather. Only now do I realise how much I disliked the old one.

Three years ago we drove a standard Vanquish over this road and it didn't acquit itself too well. At speeds that would barely have woken some rivals' chassis it bottomed out and became very lively. It was an 80 per cent car. This version is a 90 per cent car. It controls its mass so much better, changes direction with more commitment and accuracy. It is also much more accelerative. An altered differential ratio makes as much of a performance difference as the added power and torque, perhaps more. Aston claims 9.8sec to

100mph, and that's probably a little on the cautious side. There's no reason to doubt the claimed 200mph top speed.

The engine seems smoother, too. Mechanical refinement has never been a weakness, but from idle to the 7200rpm limiter this is John Travolta-slick. You spend more time delving into the power plateau, too: above 4000rpm (with the secondary exhaust valves trumpeting a noise that you just wouldn't credit from Siamese Ford Duratec V6s) it provides reason enough for many people to choose Aston over Ferrari. The only problem is that you leave all the commotion behind, so you have to lower the windows to hear it yourself.

Downshifts are excellent: timed to perfection and hardly disrupting the car's chosen line, but going up through the 'box – which you'd assume was an easier activity – isn't so great. The shifts seem ponderously slow and even when in sport mode they aren't anything like fast enough to justify the harshness.

But in other areas the Vanquish deals with Aston's current predilection for heavy controls better than the DB9 does. Because this is a more robust, speed-driven experience, the heavy brake pedal is more in keeping with the overall character. They're decent stoppers, too: 378mm front discs clamped by a six-piston caliper and 330mm (same as before but 2mm wider) out back. They do fade considerably under duress, but if you adjust the pressure applied accordingly they continue to work.

It's a compelling car, the Vanquish S. I've driven much faster, more competent machinery, but very few that I've disliked giving back as much as this. The changes are subtle; the cumulative effect they reap more significant than I'd expected. Depreciation aside, it would be a delight to wake up every morning with a Vanquish S on your driveway and know that it now drives almost as well as it looks. They just need to get Brunel to look at those upshifts.

LEFT Brakes uprated but still fade during hard use – blame the hefty 1835kg kerbweight; winged bucket seats more supportive.

LEFT Fastest-ever Aston hits 200mph: £11k over standard Vanquish buys beefed-up looks and better handling; shame the gearbox is still so slow.

DB9 ACROSS EUROPE

This feature is Peter Robinson's last as European editor of *Autocar* – and what better way to celebrate than a blast across the continent in this year's best-looking new car, the Aston Martin DB9

Any Aston Martin enthusiast hoping to stay at L'Hotel de France for the '05 Le Mans weekend is too late. The charming, if modest, little hotel in La Chartre sur le Loir, 40km south of Le Mans, home to Aston Martin's racing team during the halcyon days of the '50s, is already booked out.

For 11 years, including 1959 when Roy Salvadori and Carroll Shelby scored Aston's only Le Mans victory, John Wyer and the Aston team based themselves here. It was here, too, that the great English team manager took the Ford GT and the JW Automotive Engineering Gulf teams during their (mostly) successful sorties in the '60s. And it was to the same unassuming hotel that we ended a 1300-mile journey that began near Brescia, Italy.

I wanted an excuse for a serious drive in a production DB9 and Aston's return to Le Mans for the 24-hour race, with the DBR9 GT, provided the perfect rationale. Let me explain, on two other fronts. In the months after Aston Martin's beautiful DB9 was launched to near-universal press and prospective customer acclaim, reality set in. Expectations heightened to unsustainable levels, longer experience during comparison tests revealed the gorgeous new Aston wasn't quite the perfection implied in a number of drive stories. After suffering dramas with two DB9s, it was obvious there were quality issues that needed resolving. I determined to find a reason to spend a week with a later-build DB9.

News of Aston's long-rumoured return to the Sarthe circuit triggered memories of a connection with the Mille Miglia, Italy's great sports car race. After the Second World War, to attract more of the Le Mans field to the Mille Miglia, the classic open road Brescia-Rome-Brescia event, founder Aymo Maggi instituted a major new trophy. With the help of celebrated French journalist Charles Faroux, Maggi inaugurated the now almost forgotten Le Mans-Mille Miglia Cup, to be awarded to the driver with the best aggregate position from both races. The Cup ran from 1952 to 1956,

FEATURE

21 DECEMBER 2004

Volume 242

No 12 | 5619

adding in the Nürburgring 1000km in 1957, the last year of the Mille Miglia.

There's more. In 1951 John Wyer, who ran Aston Martin's racing team, entered two DB2s in the Mille Miglia. As he explains in his wonderfully forthright book *The Certain Sound*, the entire team was invited by Count Maggi to be guests at Casa Maggi, his estate in Calino, about 20km from Brescia, for the race. This, too, became tradition. Why not, therefore, drive a DB9 from Calino to Le Mans and stay at the Hotel de France?

Aston happily provided a royal blue, automatic (a manual doesn't go on sale until early 2005) production DB9. With photographer Stan Papior flying into Milan, I snapped the car at the gates to Casa Maggi – my friend Camilla, Aymo's widow, died at the age of 94 earlier this year, and access to the house and garages, that once housed DB3Ss, is now

difficult – before collecting him from the airport. From Milan, we planned to head north beside the eastern shores of Lake Como to the Stelvio Pass, through Austria and into Germany, reaching Le Mans by a long-cut that took in Spa, where an Aston Martin prototype won a 24-hour sports car race in 1948, and then south into France, skirting the edge of Paris on our way to Le Mans.

Italy is on holiday, the Monday autostrada traffic is thin. The Aston cruises effortlessly at 90mph, tacho needle hovering barely above idle at 2500rpm, though in the bright sunlight the instruments are hard to read. Five days' worth of luggage and camera gear has spilled over onto the tiny near-useless rear seats. Sitting so low, windscreen beyond reach, I'm surprised at how much bigger, especially wider, the DB9 feels than a Porsche 911. Visibility is limited, the view through the rear screen distorted by some fault

'THE 444BHP-LED PERFORMANCE BUILDS IN HARMONY WITH A TYPICALLY V12 EXHAUST BELLOW'

in the glass manufacturing. And, because the power steering is much heavier, it lacks the Porsche's innate agility. It takes no more than a few miles to understand the DB9 is more GT than sports car. If next year's shorter-wheelbase V8 Vantage is more sporty, Aston's positioning of the two models couldn't be better.

Papior would be in paradise, if he could get the DB9 down to the water's edge. We've meandered beside the villas that separate the road from Lake Como, frustrated not to find car access to the lake. Finally, close to the northern end, we strike lucky. A narrow lane takes us down to a small point jutting out into the water. It's wide enough for a car, but a bollard prevents access to a slipway on the stony beach, but there's a ramshackle row of the kind of evocative houses photographers love. When an old woman begins hanging out washing from her window, Papior has the near perfect Italian-cliche photograph.

Our presence attracts the curiosity of a well-dressed, middle-aged Italian male. How many cylinders, what engine capacity? He claims to have a Lamborghini Miura SS in Milan. Having agreed that the DB9 deserves comparison with the Miura, the world's most beautiful car, we shake hands. After asking why we were not photographing the Aston by the lake, our new friend walks up to the bollard and lifts it out of the ground. Local knowledge. Manoeuvring the

Aston for the camera, I'm conscious of the throttle's sudden initial movement, an on-off lunging action that hampers gentle progress. And not for the last time, I scrape the car's under-spoiler chin. Aston hasn't yet eliminated the steering-wheel judder that annoyed me on the pre-production launch cars. I'm also having trouble finding my way round the console's too-small controls, and whinge at the CD-satellite navigation's tardy performance.

Following a bowl of pasta by the lake, it's time for serious driving into the Alps. After cruising at moderate revs in sixth, way below the 5000rpm torque peak, the level of sheer grunt in the lower gears at higher rpm comes as a shock. A single tap of the left paddle converts the brilliant six-speed torque-convertor automatic into manual mode. The 444bhp-led performance builds in harmony with a typically V12 exhaust bellow and (from 3800rpm) induction roar that is so intoxicating, you can't help but drop down a gear or three before accelerating hard in tunnels to hear the sound echoing between the walls, filling the cabin with a sound so inspired that we yell with delight. So accessible is the acceleration, so velvety the drivetrain in both fully auto and manual modes, and so bullying the sound, that the Aston's crushingly swift performance seemingly intimidates any potential rivals.

ABOVE DB9 on the prowl; a beautiful car, a beautiful village... and a woman hanging out washing; author Robinson takes the wheel for his transcontinental odyssey.

OPPOSITE Beautiful, isn't it? And the scenery around Lake Como's not bad.

ABOVE Stelvio Pass once world's highest road; has 94 hairpin bends.

RIGHT Make sure you select 'Drive': precipitous roads no place for errors.

RIGHT Incredible roads perfect for DB9.

FAR RIGHT Book your ferry now. Roads like these demand to be driven on.

Until 1936, the 2757-metre serpentine Stelvio Pass was the highest road in the world. With 48 hairpin corners on the Austrian side and 46 coming from Italy, the Stelvio was also famous, until a decade ago, as the ultimate brake-testing location. But during the short summer period when the pass is open, there's now so much traffic the brake engineers have moved elsewhere in the Alps. Understandable, given the volume of camper-vans, caravans, hat-wearing Volvo drivers and even buses we encountered. The only vehicles making real progress are the squadrons of superbikes. Oh, and a trio of aggressively driven, Munich-registered, 911s. Don't be put off: arrive early in the morning, or after 6.00pm in the evening, and the road is virtually traffic free, instantly becoming one of driving's most inspired and challenging routes. Be warned: a couple of the Italian tunnels are one lane only, include unlit blind corners, and function without a contra-flow system. Dangerous in the extreme.

In August, finding free rooms in an hotel in Italy proves impossible, so headlights ablaze we head further north into Austria. In Nauders, the first town across the border, we immediately find beds.

The following morning an electrical glitch claims that the fuel tank is empty, despite the trip computer maintaining we have 362km of range left. Switching off and restarting, doesn't help. Distance to empty now reads zero.

As a precaution we refuel. The 85-litre tank is brimmed after accepting just 28 litres. A few kilometres down the road the trip-computer corrects itself and behaves perfectly for the rest of our journey, except the computer insists our average speed fluctuates between 91mph and 221mph.

Austria's roads are smooth and quiet, the DB9 sits four-square, swallowing distances, stringing sweepers together more by instinct than any conscious wheel movement, despite a leaden on-centre feel that helps create the impression the all-alloy Aston is excessively heavy. The weighting of the major controls – the brakes, too, require a substantial shove – reflect Aston boss Ulrich Bez's personal taste.

I'd hoped to explore the DB9's 186mph v-max on the autobahn running north to Ulm, but holiday traffic stifles the idea. A couple of hours later, on a new section of the E42 motorway, north of Trier towards Spa/Liege, the Aston find its legs and cruises for a few minutes at 150mph, hitting 170mph in fifth before the onset of aerodynamic factors begins to appreciably slow the rate of acceleration. What we learn is that the Aston is faster in fifth than it is in the super-high-geared sixth. Nor is the DB9 quiet at these speeds. The build-up in road and wind roar almost drowns out the now hard-working V12.

The highlight of our overnight stay, close to the famous Spa circuit, is eating in the same restaurant as some BAR F1 transport drivers. Unfortunately the entire circuit was closed to private transport the next morning. As recently as eight years ago, Eau Rouge was part of the commuter route for a number of locals. Then, the spectator sport was watching VW Golf GTis, Renault Clio Williams and Renault 21 Turbos belt down past the pits, hitting the cut-out on every gearchange, to take motor racing's best corner flat out (well, flat by hot-hatch standards). The occasional spin and blown engine always enlivened the action.

'THE SERPENTINE STELVIO PASS IS ONE OF DRIVING'S MOST INSPIRED AND CHALLENGING DRIVING ROUTES'

RIGHT Overlooking Eau Rouge at Spa.

RIGHT Nothing but deserted grandstands and ruined buildings at Reims circuit.

BELOW DB9's graceful lines are as inspiring as its throaty soundtrack.

Sadly, that's all finished now: a bypass takes all regular traffic away from the circuit and Eau Rouge is closed. Still, Papior noticed a small track through the surrounding forests. Gingerly crawling along the gravel trail, the Aston nosed out into a small clearing in front of the grandstand and directly above the great corner. After a lap of the original 8.7-mile road circuit – and a photo at the famous Masta kink, where once Porsche 917s and Ferrari 512Ss hit over 200mph on the two-lane blacktop between farm houses – we pointed the Aston towards Paris. And hoped the bum ache, induced on firm bucket seats that were becoming harder with every mile, wouldn't increase. It didn't, but softer cushions would be welcome.

We agreed it would petulant not to leave the autoroute and spend a few minutes paying homage at the partially restored grandstand and pits of the old Reims race track, last used for the French Grand Prix in 1966, when Jack Brabham won. As part of the local campaign to save what's left of the circuit, the old structures carry signs asking us to, 'Remember the pilots' and 'Respect of the site'.

The rain storm that slowed traffic to a walk on

ABOVE Old Reims
race track last used
for the 1966 French
Grand Prix.

the outer Paris ring road didn't worry the Aston. No aquaplaning, no hesitation from the brakes, effective wipers and demisting, the rear screen staying perfectly clear once above 25mph, due solely to the airflow over the glass. Things you could never take for granted from supercars less than a decade ago.

The navigation system led the DB9 to the main square of La Chartre sur le Loir, and there was the hotel. The tiny rooms, decorated '60s style, don't do the two-star justice. The food is brilliant, the dining room delightful, but for Aston fans it's the bar, decorated with old racing souvenirs and photographs, that stirs the imagination. My favourite: a shot of Carroll Shelby, Maurice Trintignant and Stirling Moss playing cards. Ask to see the scrapbook that's kept high above reception. This contains clippings that trace the story of Wyer's teams' annual visits to the hotel. We washed the car by hand in the little courtyard behind the hotel, because that's where the Aston mechanics cleaned the cars 50 years ago.

Drive the Le Mans circuit, as we did the following morning, and there's a perception of a race track being used as a road, rather than the opposite. Despite two chicanes, intended to slow the competitors, it's obvious the Mulsanne straight remains one of the fastest sections of race track in the world. Here, effectively our journey was over,

though we were still committed to returning the DB9 to Aston's HQ at Gaydon, Warwickshire.

What, then, are we to make of this fine GT car? As of our drive in August, there were still small, niggly, issues to be resolved, but after a tour of the impressive Gaydon assembly line and an inspection of the then-current production cars, I'm convinced cures are in place for most of them. It's a given that nobody can fail to be moved by the Aston's graceful beauty. But that's no longer the only reason to buy a DB9. I'm convinced the car would benefit from a general lightening of the major controls, yet it remains an excellent long-distance tourer: a hard-to-believe overall 19.3mpg from a 6.0-litre V12 owes plenty to the relaxed gearing. The basics are thoroughly well-developed, the interior (if not the dashboard) is elegant and welcoming. I expected the firm ride to be an issue, but only when we crossed the channel did we become aware of the chassis' limitations. Strange that the ride on English roads, where the DB9 spent most of its development time, is worse than on European routes, including Belgium's poorly maintained bitumen.

This is a car for Continental motoring, where the V12 and that terrific chassis can play to their many strengths. It's worth buying one, just to be a part of next year's Le Mans. Wonder if there's a free table at L'Hotel over the weekend?

ASTON VANQUISH S

It might look identical to the standard car, but with more power and an enhanced chassis the S is the fastest and best Vanquish – and Aston – ever

In many ways the Vanquish S is the supreme proof of how serious a player Aston Martin is in 2005. On the surface the 'new improved' Vanquish S looks much the same as the car that was launched to critical acclaim in 2001. It remains the definitive big Aston: as beautiful as it is brutal and as quintessentially British as roast beef and Yorkshire pud.

But in reality this new S version of Aston's most expensive car is a very different machine. It has 60bhp more, a much-improved chassis, bigger brakes and a tastefully redesigned interior.

And that's precisely why the Vanquish S proves what it does about AM's present state of mind. Aston could easily have left the Vanquish alone and spent the money somewhere else. Sales were still strong and no one could deny that the Vanquish continues to do the business in terms of appearance. But instead Aston chose to throw time and money at the car's engineering yet had the temerity to leave the visuals well alone. That takes confidence, not to mention determination and a certain clarity of thought.

DESIGN AND ENGINEERING ★★★★☆
Evolution of an already strong package

The Vanquish S is the fastest car ever to wear those famous Aston wings; the official top speed is now in excess of 200mph. All the body panels are fashioned

QUICK FACTS

Model tested	Vanquish S
List price	£174,000
Top speed	200+mph
30–70mph	4.8sec
0–60mph	47.7m
70–0mph	46.8m
Average test MPG	13.4
For	Sense of occasion
Against	Pricey, limited range

ROAD TEST

17 MAY 2005

Volume 244

No 7 | 5639

JAPAN'S JAG New Lexus GS meets (and beats) real thing

AUTOCAR

1000-MILE SHOOTOUT

3500 Quality Car's Index

For the 9th and final time

NEW EVO

Sub £30k heroes... A to B just got quicker

« FASTEST-EVER ASTON
Full test of astonishing Vanquish S

AUDI'S BABY LIMO »
Top-secret luxury city car revealed

ROAD TEST VANQUISH S

MAXIMUM SPEEDS

6th 200+mph **5th** 169mph/7200rpm
4th 135/7200 **3rd** 103/7200
2nd 75/7200 **1st** 51/7200

ACCELERATION FROM REST

True mph	seconds	speedo mph
30	2.2	30
40	2.9	40
50	3.9	51
60	4.8	62
70	5.8	72
80	7.3	83
90	8.6	94
100	10.1	104
110	12.2	115
120	14.1	125
130	–	–
140	–	–
150	–	–

Standing qtr mile 13.1sec/114.8mph
Standing km 21.9sec/153mph
30–70mph through gears 3.6sec

ACCELERATION IN GEAR

MPH	6th	5th	4th	3rd	2nd
20–40	-	-	-	-	2.2
30–50	-	-	3.7	2.9	2.1
40–60	-	5.1	3.7	2.8	2.1
50–70	6.6	5.1	3.6	2.8	2.0
60–80	7.2	5.1	3.7	2.8	–
70–90	7.5	5.3	3.8	2.8	–
80–100	7.3	5.4	3.9	–	–
90–110	7.4	5.4	–	–	–
100–120	–	5.3	–	–	–
110–130	–	–	–	–	–
120–140	–	–	–	–	–
130–150	–	–	–	–	–

FUEL CONSUMPTION

Average/best/worst/touring
13.4/5.6/19.4mpg

Urban/combined	10.1/16.9mpg
Tank capacity	80 litres
Theoretical range	297 miles
Real-world range	230 miles

BRAKES

30/50/70mph 9.2/24.7/47.7 metres
60-0mph 2.9sec
Pedal feel poor/fair/**good**/excellent
Fade poor/**fair**/good/excellent

HANDLING AND RIDE

Normal driving
Balance understeer/oversteer/**neutral**
Steering feel poor/fair/**good**/excellent
Body control poor/fair/**good**/excellent
Ride quality poor/fair/good/**excellent**
Grip poor/fair/**good**/excellent

Hard driving
Balance understeer/**oversteer**/neutral
Steering feel poor/**fair**/good/excellent
Body control poor/**fair**/good/excellent
Ride quality poor/fair/**good**/excellent
Grip poor/fair/**good**/excellent

Test notes Could do with more body
control at high speeds, but the trade
off is exceptional low speed ride for a
200mph supercar.

NOISE

Idle/max revs in 3rd 52/91dbA
30/50/70mph 67/69/75dbA
Sound quality poor/fair/good/**excellent**

HEADLIGHTS

Dipped beam poor/fair/**good**/excellent
Full beam poor/fair/**good**/excellent
Test notes Good spread of light.

from aluminium, the 6.0-litre V12 has been massaged to produce a thumping 520bhp at 7000rpm and the chassis/suspension/braking/steering have all received numerous upgrades over those of the original Vanquish which, incidentally, remains on sale for £163,600.

The big news concerns the engine. Thanks to new cylinder heads, a revised ECU, more highly polished inlet ports, better fuel injectors and forged conrods, the 5935cc V12 now produces an extra 60bhp and 25lb ft (making 520bhp and 425lb ft in total) though these peaks are attained slightly higher in the rev range.

At the same time, the gearing has been lowered. Together with the increases in power and torque this, says Aston, shaves nearly two seconds from the

PERFORMANCE/BRAKES ★★★★☆
Aston's fastest-ever car. Pity about brake fade

Our normal test track (Millbrook) was not available, so we used another that does not have as much grip. You therefore need almost to ignore the 0–60mph time of 4.8sec, because by then the S was barely into its stride in terms of traction. This explains why it was seemingly four-tenths slower to 60mph than the regular Vanquish, which we figured at 4.4sec.

A far better clue as to how much quicker the S is than its lesser sibling is the 0–100mph time; even on a poor surface it managed 10.0sec compared with 10.4sec for the regular model. Slice half a second from that (which would come with a grippier surface) and you're looking at around 9.5sec to 100mph, or a second quicker than the standard car and well into Ferrari F430/ Porsche 911 Turbo territory.

The Vanquish has never been primarily about raw numbers, however, even though it can now churn these out with the best of them. What's more important by far is the character it exudes and the noise it makes, and it's hard to think of any rival that can match it in these areas, especially since the way you access the performance is now so much clearer thanks to a much-improved paddle-shift gearbox.

For the eruption of sound that occurs as the crank spins past 3000rpm alone, the Vanquish is more endearing in many ways than any current Ferrari save, perhaps, the F430. But when mixed with this level of throttle response above 3500rpm, this much acceleration over the last 1500rpm and this much torque across the rev range, the S makes a compelling case for itself beside any rival, at any price.

Softly sprung, making for a supple ride, but handling control still excellent; more GT than hard-core sportster.

50–70mph time in top. In other words, the S isn't just slightly quicker; it's much quicker.

The chassis is the other area in which Aston has focused its efforts. There are stiffer springs and dampers, a 20 per cent faster steering rack and bigger front brake discs with six-pot calipers. The ride height has also been lowered by 5mm.

You'd need to be something of a Vanquish aficionado to spot the tiny new front splitter and the slightly higher lip on the boot lid, but together these reduce the Cd from 0.33 to 0.32. What you won't fail to spot, however, is the new interior. The original Vanquish was criticised for its Ford-influenced cabin; the S has had a full makeover and is now far more in keeping, style-wise, with the DB9, right down to the new, more supportive seats.

WHAT IT COSTS

ASTON MARTIN VANQUISH S	
On-the-road price	£174,000
Price as tested	£180,325
CO$_2$	448g/km
Tax at 22/40% pcm	£1117/£2030
Cost per mile	na
Contract hire/month	na

INSURANCE

Insurance/typical quote	20/£809

WARRANTY

Three years/60,000 miles

EQUIPMENT CHECKLIST	
Air conditioning	■
Traction control	■
Electric seats	■
Leather trim	■
Sat-nav	£1750
Rear seats	£4000
Heated seats	£295
Rear parking sensors	£250
Six-disc CD autochanger	■

Options in **bold** fitted to test car
■ = Standard na = not available

SPECIFICATIONS VANQUISH S

DIMENSIONS

Front legroom 910/1100mm Front headroom 850/900mm Boot volume 170 litres
Boot width min/max 870/1260mm Boot length 960mm Boot height 580mm
Kerbweight (claimed) 1878kg Weight distribution front:rear na
Front/rear tracks 1572/1584mm Width (inc mirrors) 1998mm

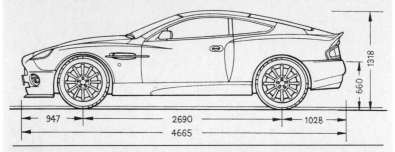

947   2690   1028
4665

1318
660

ENGINE

Layout	V12, 5295cc
Power	520bhp at 7000rpm
Torque	425lb ft at 5800rpm
Max engine speed	7200rpm
Specific output	88bhp per litre
Power to weight	283bhp per tonne*
Torque to weight	232lb ft per tonne*
Installation	Front, longitudinal, rear-wheel drive
Construction	Alloy head & block
Bore/stroke	89.0/79.5mm
Valve gear	4 per cyl, quad ohc
Compression ratio	10.8:1
Management	Visteon

TRANSMISSION

Gearbox 6-speed automated manual
Ratios/mph per 1000rpm
Final drive ratio 4.30

1st	2.664/7.0	2nd	1.783/10.5
3rd	1.302/14.4	4th	1.00/18.7
5th	0.80/23.5	6th	0.63/29.8

CHASSIS AND BODY

Body	Two-door coupé, steel unibody construction with aluminium panels
Wheels	Alloy F/R 9J × 19in/10J × 19in
Tyres	F/R Yokohama 255/40 ZR19, 285/40 ZR19
Safety	Driver and passenger airbags

STEERING

Type Rack and pinion, speed-sensitive hydraulic power assistance
Turns lock-to-lock 2.1
Turning circle na

SUSPENSION

Front Double wishbones, coil springs, anti-roll bar
Rear Double wishbones, coil springs, anti-roll bar

BRAKES

Front 378mm ventilated discs
Rear 330mm ventilated discs
Anti-lock Standard, with electronic brakeforce distribution

*Power- and torque-to-weight figures calculated using manufacturer's claimed kerb weight. The performance figures were taken with the odometer reading 2450 miles. Autocar test results are protected by world copyright and may not be reproduced without the editor's written permission

---

But it's a pity it doesn't stop better. Actually that's not fair; it stops very well – for a while. Then, inevitably, fade soon sets in. Allowed to cool the brakes come back but, there's not a lot more you can do to control 520bhp, 200mph and 1878kg.

HANDLING AND RIDE ★★★★
Softer than you'd think but beautifully refined

Despite stiffer springs and dampers and a faster steering rack, the first time you drive the S hard over a good road you think it's not sharp enough. Not enough body control, too little rear suspension composure on turn in, too much effort required to keep it on the straight and narrow. And the first time you grind the nose into the floor on the south side of a large undulation, you even begin to wonder whether there might be something amiss; it's that softly suspended.

And yet the more time you spend with the Vanquish S, the more you begin to appreciate the suspension set-up. After 500 miles we almost completely revised our opinion on it, and the reason we did so was the ride, which is sensationally good.

What Aston has created is not a cutting-edge sports car but a comfortable GT that will, if pushed, corner hard enough and crisply enough for 99 per cent of drivers. True, it does begin to move around somewhat if you venture beyond the limits of the grippy Yokohama tyres or the surprisingly soft suspension, but even then the only real risk is thumping the nose into the floor and losing a bit of paint. Even in extremis it's a delightfully benign handler.

It steers nicely, too, albeit in a slightly artificial kind of way. The new rack is quicker and initially seems more precise, but it doesn't actually contain more feel and the lack of lock in tight spaces is a step backwards. Overall it's an 85 per cent steering system attached to a 90 per cent chassis. Pretty damn good, in other words.

SAFETY AND EQUIPMENT ★★★★★
Big improvement over the original interior

Accept the fact that it is very much a two-plus-one-and-a-half in terms of rear seat space and there's not a lot else you can fault this car on in this section. The new cabin is a massive step up from the original; from the new be-winged sports seats to the gorgeous new door inserts to the smell of the Bridge of Weir leather that greets you the moment you climb aboard, the S exudes that rare atmosphere only a genuine exotic

can give off. It feels impossibly expensive and is now exceptionally well made.

It's also stacked with every conceivable goodie that a wealthy owner would expect (including a bespoke Linn hi-fi), except for a sat-nav system or TV. The latter is not available; the former will unfortunately cost you a little extra, sir.

Active safety is strong, with traction control and anti-lock brakes as standard but, interestingly, there are no stability control or brake-assist systems. Neither were greatly missed during our 500 miles with the car.

RUNNING COSTS ★
Expensive car that's more expensive to run

You don't buy a £174,000 Aston Martin and worry greatly about its running costs, but for what it's worth they're pretty horrendous. Depreciation is the biggest worry – and it starts the moment you take delivery. A four-year-old S might well be worth less than six figures.

Relative to this, an overall test figure of 13.4mpg hardly seems worth worrying about, nor the group 20 insurance and 35 per cent company car tax rates.

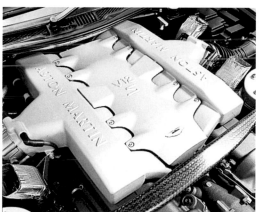

ABOVE Interior quality much improved; steering quicker, more precise; Linn hi-fi sounds good, but not as good as the engine.

LEFT 6.0-litre V12 now produces 520bhp.

AUTOCAR VERDICT

Since its launch in 2001 the Vanquish has always been an impossibly endearing machine, the perfect example of the modern-day big, hairy Aston. But this new S version goes one better than that. Not only is it faster and therefore hairier than ever on paper, in reality it's also more refined, far better to sit in, more comfortable and just plain better to drive, period. Vitally, it also distances itself sufficiently from the DB9 to make sense as a stand-alone model at the top of Aston Martin's increasingly impressive range of cars. Warts and all, we think it's fabulous.

The most desirable Aston ever　　★★★★☆

OPEN, ALL OURS

DB9 VOLANTE Well, for a day at least, and that's all the time Adam Towler has to find out if the new open-top Aston Martin DB9 is made of the same stuff as the coupé

One thousand miles were etched on the face looking back at me. Hard miles. It had started at 4.45am on a cold, dark, foggy morning deep in the English countryside 18 months ago. Outside my house was a dark blue DB9 coupé that was due in Italy for a big group test with the Ferrari 612 and Bentley Continental GT the next day.

And if that wasn't enough, *Autocar* needed some performance figures, so it was timing gear, Millbrook proving ground and 0–160mph before breakfast, followed by the British rush hour, the *Pride of Calais* reverberating to a V12 in its hull by late morning, and then France, beaten into the rear-view mirror by dusk. Then the hairpins on the climb up to the Mont Blanc tunnel – negotiated with the cackle of blipped downshifts – and the hallucinogenic streaming of endless tunnels across the border on the blisteringly fast run downhill past Aosta. Then finally to that mirror, in a nondescript hotel room at a quarter to midnight, and a face so heavily drawn as to be almost unrecognisable as my own. The next morning I took a photo of the DB9's face, which I still have: it's the best bug collection you've ever seen. It took hard work to accrue that lot.

I haven't been in a DB9 since the crazy few days of that test – which, incidentally, the DB9 coupé

went on to win – but today should be very different. Today is about basking in the sun, about enjoying the sweeping country lanes of middle England, appreciating this green and pleasant land, the sight of grazing cows, fields of corn and quaint cottages, the sound of chirping birds. Maybe a pot of tea, even a scone or two. The Volante is different, you see. It's that sort of car. Time to take it a bit easier.

A convertible model was planned right from the start of the DB9 project – a task made easier by the advanced aluminium chassis that enables fundamental changes to be made. But the DB9 convertible is more than just a roofless coupé; it's really a whole new model, developed with a different kind of Aston buyer in mind. A DB9 engineer used the ungainly phrase 'boulevard cruiser', but it gives you the idea. It's not hard to see what Aston is looking for here, and it's not the long, repetitive 'boulevards' of central Milton Keynes. The company expects 70 per cent of DB9s sold in the USA to be Volante models. So there are softer springs front and rear, and less aggressive damping. There's no point getting down on your hands and knees and peering underneath for a rear anti-roll bar because you won't find one, and the front bar is smaller.

Remarkably little has been done to put back some of the chassis rigidity lost by guillotining the DB9's roof: there's a shear panel bolted to the underside over much of the front half of the car and the chassis' sill sections are made from slightly thicker aluminium, but are otherwise the same. The upshot of this is that the convertible is only 60kg heavier than the coupé. To help prevent any unfortunate incidents that may lead to your toupee parting company with your tanned head, Aston limits the top speed of the Volante to 'just' 165mph.

The theatre ingrained within the Volante begins the moment you set eyes on it. Crucially, it is at this moment – apart from on start-up, perhaps – that the Volante delivers its winning line, its killer

QUICK FACTS

Model	DB9 Volante
Price	£115,000
On sale	May 2005
Top speed	186mph
0–60mph	4.9sec
MPG	tbc
CO$_2$ emissions	394g/km
Insurance group	20
Engine	V12, 5935cc
Power	450bhp at 6000rpm
Torque	420lb ft at 5000rpm

FIRST DRIVE

24 MAY 2005

Volume 244

No 8 I 5640

catchphrase. It's rare for a modern car to have such a purity of line that you're left simply standing and staring. For minutes. Perhaps the cleverest thing about the DB9, and the Volante as much as the coupé, is that without resorting to any retro cheesiness it completely avoids the shock tactics that some manufacturers deem necessary to create visual impact. It simply looks magnificent: a blend of British power, prestige, athleticism and gilt-edged affluence to steal the show anywhere in the world.

And it keeps on grabbing your attention the closer you get to it, with real depth to the details such as the elegant flip-out door handles, the beautifully integrated xenon light units, the bold side strakes over the open vents and a glossy paint finish and precision of panel fit well in keeping with the £115,000 price. Considering the sudden appearance of the sun, it seems only fitting to lower the canvas roof, a task that's fully automatic after the toggling of a switch on the right of the centre console. In 17

seconds the roof whirs away behind its tonneau, leaving the two small humps from where the roll-bars blast out when a roll-over incident is deemed imminent. All very slick.

Twist the ignition key until the dash glows and thumb the button to start the 450bhp 6.0-litre V12. Time for part two of the Volante's stage-show noise. Although the chugga-chugga-chugga ka-BOOM is the same as the coupé's, without the insulation of a roof it's all the more immediate and spectacular. Select drive, release the occasionally awkward fly-off handbrake and you're away – with a lurch if you're not sensitive with the throttle over the first few yards. Now we're bumbling around the Warwickshire lanes near Aston's HQ and all the DB9 essentials are there as I remember them: the slightly contrived but grin-inducing 'blat' from the exhaust over 4000rpm, the heavy steering and brake pedal, firm ride and excellent gearbox – a proper slusher, but with an uncannily good

'IT'S RARE FOR A MODERN CAR TO HAVE SUCH A PURITY OF LINE THAT YOU'RE LEFT SIMPLY STANDING & STARING'

Sleek lines are complemented by the DB9's delectable detailing and beautiful finish – especially the paint.

paddle-shift function complete with throttle blips on downchanges.

Life seems sweet behind the wheel of a DB9 Volante on a summer day with the roof down. Just replacing one of the elegant new multi-spoke alloys would cripple my finances to the point of extinction, so I can only draw conjecture as to what it must be like to have casually stumped up the cash for one, finely tailored to exactly your own specification. Smug probably doesn't even begin to cover it. In fact, so blatantly flashy is the Volante that there are times when I cringe at the attention it draws. Safe to say, if you're thinking of ordering one you'll need to be an exhibitionist who loves to bask in the attention of others, and I guess that's an acquired taste.

We're heading towards Newport Pagnell, but not to visit the old works where the Vanquish is still made. Rather, we're off to a small and very English market town called Olney and the workshops of Desmond J Smail, specialist in the restoration and servicing of classic Aston Martins. Principally, because I want to see the Volante in the light of some of its predecessors, and hear the views of those who work on the old cars as to whether the new cars are 'real' Astons. Tucked away in a small courtyard is a

ABOVE Top Fascia looks good and for the most part the quality is a long way ahead of many of Aston's previous offerings. Only the switches on the dash let it down.

LEFT Cabin is snug, and the seats are supportive and very comfortable.

LEFT Rear seats are vestigial, to put it mildly – you'd struggle to fit a toddler in here.

ABOVE The Volante isn't really cut out for enthusiastic cornering; it feels too heavy, but it's explosively quick on the straights.

OPPOSITE DB9 Volante lines up in Aston Martin specialist Desmond Smail's yard, alongside the timeless DB5.

collection of brick workshops, and as the Volante prods in with its long nose from the corner of the square it meets a collection of classic DBs. There's a silver DB5 on axle stands having its gearbox removed and a forget-me-not blue DB5 slowly rusting to oblivion, awaiting a patient owner with a handy quarter of a million burning a hole in their pocket.

The big shock is immediate: the DB9 Volante is a spectacular car, a supremely stylish car. But it is not a truly beautiful car. Where it had looked feline and graceful, it now looks merely purposeful beside the feminine DB5 with its fabulous curves and classical proportions. It can't hope to compete with the way the light licks seductively over the Five's vented bonnet and dances around the pontoon wings. You can't really criticise Aston Martin for this – there's no doubt which car you'd rather be in in a crash, which car would last longer and which is the more aerodynamic, but it does put some of my earlier musings into perspective.

It's not long before two of Smail's mechanics are poring over the new arrival. There's praise for the shape, and love for the noise. Less happy is the reaction to the interior. The new piano black fascia

gets the thumbs-up, but the switches on the dash 'look like one of those cheap radios from Tesco.' The key – an old Jaguar item – produces howls of laughter and some of the niggles like the poorly closing boot get a frown. I hadn't even considered the Ford parentage of the V12 – fundamentally two Duratec V6s spliced together – as an issue, but to these guys it is, and they bemoan the lack of a homegrown unit like the classic straight-six and V8. But the key question is, do they think it's a real Aston? 'No' is the instant reply. 'It's far too well made to be an Aston.' It's a quip made with genuine affection for the old cars, but it makes a revealing point all the same. Aston Martin has made such huge strides in quality, specification and performance that its new products seem divorced from what came before, with just enough heritage to keep the marque true to itself.

Finally, with all the photos in the bag, there's time for a proper drive. You can instantly feel that the Volante is more laid-back than the coupé. The primary ride is thankfully softer than the uncompromising coupé's, but the secondary ride still isn't good enough and there's noticeable bodyroll when you turn into a corner enthusiastically. One of the odd sensations you get driving a DB9 – magnified in the Volante – is how much car is in front of you and how much inertia you have to overcome before you can really turn into a corner. You sit low, with acres of dashboard stretching out in front of you and a mass of bonnet after that, hidden from view. As such, the car seems to pivot from a point some way ahead of the driver's seat and you're always aware in slower corners of the weight of the V12 up front. The steering is heavy initially, but once you've turned into a corner the car feels as if it's understeering early and in a pronounced way, only to regain its composure and grip keenly around a corner from there on.

Everything changes for the better when you get back on the throttle, as the nose-heavy sensation fades and the Volante sits down and powers its way determinedly out of a curve. It really is explosively quick down the straights, given a chance to use the full rev range, but you can't help feeling you're trying to force the car to do something it really rather wouldn't – push it hard and things quickly get a bit ragged. The bottom line is slightly uncomfortable but true: you'll have more fun on your favourite B-road in a decent hot hatch than you will in a Volante.

Heading home with the roof up the Volante's appeal starts to wear a bit thin. There's surprising shake through the steering wheel and shimmer from the A-pillars over bumps. More wind noise than you'd expect through the hood, too. It just doesn't have the tight integrity of a Porsche Boxster, say, which at this price is surprising, to say the least.

The Volante, then, is an event. A glorious, A-list style event, best sampled with warm sunshine and an appreciative audience. If the DB9 coupé is emphatically Sean Connery's car in spirit, then the Volante is very much Roger Moore's. That says everything you need to know. There are those who profess Moore to be the best Bond, but they are, of course, completely wrong.

'THE VOLANTE IS A SPECTACULAR CAR, A SUPREMELY STYLISH CAR, BUT IT IS NOT A TRULY BEAUTIFUL CAR'

VANQUISHING POINT

VANQUISH S The Vanquish S, last of the old-school Astons, seduces Andrew Frankel on a 1000-mile drive from the company's past to its future

There are many ways of detecting greatness in a car, but none quite so reliable as its appearance after 500 hard and fast miles on the road. If you climb out, take one look at its mud-spattered flanks and bug-splattered nose and start casting around for a car wash, I'm afraid that while your car may or may not be any good, it is most certainly not great. But if the sight of several thousand examples of the local fauna rendered two-dimensional by the apocalyptic introduction of your car to their backsides makes you relive every last glorious mile, believe me, you have a true great on your hands.

Some cars just look better this way. And however good you may think Aston's Vanquish S looks polished to within a millimetre of its primer on a show stand, it is as nothing compared to how it looks after several hundred miles of high-speed European exercise. The hours of accumulated crap add purpose and context to what is otherwise mere beauty, to create a sight much more stirring than when it started.

Our start was in Newport Pagnell. The association of this place with Aston Martin is extraordinary, with even the road signs proclaiming it to be "the home of Aston Martin." But it's not where Aston Martin started life (Feltham) nor where most have been built (Bloxham) nor even where the HQ is today (Gaydon). Yet we all consider Newport as the marque's true home.

Our purpose was to take a Vanquish – the only car still built in Newport – and drive to Cologne where, in a very small corner of a very large Ford plant, all of Aston Martin's engine production now takes place. Having produced Astons non-stop since 1959, the Vanquish will be the last to be built in Newport Pagnell and, as I drove north from London to meet it, I wondered what former chairmen like David Brown and Victor Gauntlett would have felt about such a large part of Aston's soul now being built by the Germans.

It was great to go back. The new factory at Gaydon is magnificent but you won't find men hitting sheets of aluminium with hammers. There are no ancient lathes

FEATURE

26 JULY 2005

Volume 245

No 4 I 5649

ABOVE Vanquish hangs out with lots of other Vanquishes at Newport Pagnell.

ABOVE RIGHT At Newport, things are still done the old way; DB4 (prototype shown here) was the first production car to be built there.

or workers with pencils behind their ears, but they're still at Newport. We even managed to unearth a prototype for the DB4, the first car to go into series production there.

Those I spoke to seemed worried that the facility would be sold when legislation outlaws the Vanquish in 2008, but I have been told there are no such plans. Aston Martin is growing a service and restoration business at the old factory, where the craftsmanship can still be put to good use, so it is to be hoped that this will ensure its survival long into the future.

For now, though, I had to get to know the Vanquish again. Reacquainting yourself with such a car is like meeting an old school friend: within 10 minutes he or she will have annoyed you so much you wonder why you bothered. But as you ease into each other's company once more, so it becomes clear that the magic that sparked your relationship is still there.

Still, the Aston tried my patience. It is ridiculous that a company owned by Ford can offer for sale a £174,000 car with a poor driving position, unsupportive seats, no cruise control, ancient Jaguar switchgear and a map-free satellite navigation system. I know why: Aston produces 350 Vanquishes each year and cannot justify the level of investment required to right these issues. But that doesn't mean they don't rankle. To make matters worse, I'd driven there in a

£30k Mitsubishi Evo IX and, after that, the Aston didn't even feel very fast.

I reached the coast in heavy traffic and unimproved humour, thoughts of how much more could be achieved with a Porsche 911 Carrera S and a hundred grand in the bank now resident in my head. I never was someone who could be romanced by the look of a car alone: if the hardware beneath can't cash the cheque written by its appearance, what you have is not just a bad car, but a bad car that's betrayed your trust.

Then again, I knew this car better than that. I've managed to find an excuse to drive one at least once a year since I wrote its first road test in 2001, and every one has done its best to make me hate it, and every one has failed. I was still confident the S, with its 520bhp motor, would be no different.

It is not difficult to find Cologne from Calais – it's one of the least rewarding drives you can do. So, once I'd had my fill of autoroute and dodging Belgian police, we peeled off the motorway and swung south, drawn by the lure of Spa.

Aston Martin has no fabulous history at the legendary Ardennes circuit but the similarities between them commanded the visit. Both came into being in the early 1920s and made their names through both speed and beauty. Both were changed extensively in the 1980s but, despite being redefined for the modern era, both have managed to cling to the appeal that made them great in the first place.

Of course, the new circuit was busy, but for once I didn't mind. I took to the old track, barrelled it through Stavelot fast enough for photographer Stan to shout at me and ate chips at the Masta Friterie, next to where Pedro Rodriguez and Jo Siffert would have had to persuade their Porsche 917s to change direction twice at over 180mph. The chips weren't great but it hardly mattered. Sitting there, I was glad to have the Aston with me and not something of less noble stock. In places like this, it's important to turn up in the right wheels.

Inevitably, I stayed too long and by the time the thrumming of Stan's fingers on the table became unbearable, the light was fading fast. So, discovering the navigation system to be entirely useless, we set off cross-country to find both Germany and the true spirit of the Vanquish.

Expect the Vanquish to do it all for you and it will remain a disappointment. Unlike a DB9, the Vanquish needs to be learnt. The engine needs extending in every gear because, by upping the output from the DB9's 450bhp to 520bhp, some of the mid-range punch has been lost. And you have to figure out the paddle-actuated gearbox because, if you just tug when you feel like it, it will jolt every change. You have to time it; it is you that makes the difference.

And swiftly you learn that the more you put into this car, the more you get out. Treat it as the precision instrument that it is and it will show you talents you would never have dreamt it possessed. These include superlative body control, fabulous balance, crisp steering and, for a rear-drive car with neither engine nor gearbox over the back axle, quite exceptional traction.

One corner, whose radius opened at the same rate as the Aston accelerated, meant you could keep the

'THE MORE YOU PUT INTO THIS CAR, THE MORE YOU GET OUT. TREAT IT AS THE PRECISION INSTRUMENT THAT IT IS'

That V12 is still made by hand, despite the distinct lack of men with pencils behind their ears.

ABOVE Aston takes a turn around the (very modern) Cologne factory where its V12 is built.

OPPOSITE V12 and V8 engines in the Cologne plant waiting to be shipped to the UK; back in Newport Pagnell, the Vanquish's wings are hand-tooled; Aston is as much at home pottering along French country roads as it is blitzing the autobahn.

car on the limit and your foot on the floor all at once. And I can remember wondering whether we would run out of corner or grip first. But the Vanquish knew no such doubts and stuck to the task, pouring more and more power onto the road until we were finally straight and cannoning away from the setting sun.

Night-time coincided with the A1 autobahn, which may sound like Germany's busiest road but it was deserted. Headlights blazing, I swiftly blasted the Vanquish up to the sort of speed no road car could have looked at 20 years ago, the Aston requiring no more than a finger-tip touch. In that moment it was the absolute, undisputed master of its environment and, as I heard the V12 howling its approval, so the Vanquish reaffirmed its place in my heart.

I'll not deny that presenting ourselves at Aston Martin's latest facility the next morning induced something akin to culture shock. The Ford plant in Cologne is the city's biggest employer, with over 21,000 staff on site. It occupies an unbelievable

16 square miles of the north of the city and its main produce is the Fiesta. But tucked away in an area that used to produce Ford engines Aston motors now come together.

It's depressing at first. I found but one Brit on the premises, and not a lathe to be seen, let alone any pencils. What they do have is acres of open-plan factory, lots of walkways, clever pieces of equipment and at least one robot. Here, 95 people working at 27 stations in three shifts produce 5000 V12 and V8 engines each year for the DB9, V8 Vantage and Vanquish.

But look more closely and you'll not miss the pride of the workers. "Everyone wants to work here," says Thomas Beckert, manager of the Aston Martin engine plant. All are highly skilled and, engine-cleaning robot aside, assemble each powerplant by hand. Just 25 are finished each day while, elsewhere on site Ford V6s are produced at the rate of 2200 per day. Each Ford V6 spends 27 seconds at each work station; every Aston V12 or V8 has 12min 48sec.

'YOU CAN BUILD CARS USING BATTERED TOOLS IN A BATTERED FACTORY, AND YOU WILL GO BUST'

Look at it like this. You can return to the good old days and build cars using battered tools in a battered factory and, at their best, they will be utterly eclipsed by those that take advantage of the 21st century. At their worst they will leave your customers stranded at the side of the road, just as they did in the good old days, at which point their once manifest charms may suddenly seem rather hard to find. And you will go bust and disappear, just as Aston Martin did on too many occasions.

That era is past, and anyone who fails to recognise it will also fail in this business. But its passing doesn't mean that cars have to be any less beautiful, possess less captivating exhaust notes or less raw charm. Cars can still be fabulous to drive and, where it really matters, from the final damper specification to the cut of the leather, human beings can and will continue to make all the difference between the merely good and the truly excellent.

The Vanquish S is the bridge between these two worlds, with its extruded alloy monocoque and Ford-built motor on one side, and its hand-finished panels and construction at Newport Pagnell on the other.

But I cannot see why the next Vanquish need be any less charming for having crossed over entirely to the other side. The magic in all modern cars comes from their design and the quality of their materials; then they just have to be put together as well as humanly possible.

All of this played on my mind on the slow trudge back to London. With its fine ride and refinement, the Vanquish S had proven itself to be a great tourer and with the magnificent V12 motor allied to a now exceptional chassis, it was the car's shining talents that occupied my brain, the foibles that had so irked me on the way out now accommodated and almost forgotten. After nearly 1000 miles I was jubilant that, maybe for the last time, the Vanquish had proven my earlier misgivings so wrong.

The Vanquish S is a unique and wonderful machine. Others are more capable but, for all its faults, I can think of hardly any car made today for which I feel such raw affection. What, then, could be better than one for which no apologies need be made?

And that's what the next Vanquish must be: it won't be produced in Newport Pagnell and it'll have a German engine under the bonnet, but it stands to be not just the best Aston ever — something we've said of every one since the DB7 — but the best supercar of its era. And that's something no Aston has ever been able to claim. The opportunity is there right now; all Aston has to do is have the guts to go out and get it.

ASTON V8 VANTAGE

For Aston Martin's long-awaited new Porsche 911 rival, a new kind of *Autocar* test

The 'V8' tag once adorned the grand statesmen of the Aston Martin range; rumbling behemoths built with tender loving care in a ramble of sheds at Newport Pagnell. But just as the company has changed so radically in the past 10 years, so has the meaning of the badge. With the launch of the new V8 Vantage, the baby of the range and a major boost to production volume, the tag has come to stand for aggression, compactness and driver focus. This is a new type of Aston – and the perfect car to launch a new type of road test.

DESIGN AND ENGINEERING

The Vantage is the third car, after the Vanquish and DB9, to use Aston's VH platform – a chassis of lightweight aluminium extrusions, pressings and castings bonded and riveted together in a process similar to that used in the Lotus Elise. Previously these chassis were built by an outside contractor, but now they are constructed in-house at the spectacular new Gaydon factory in Warwickshire.

The chassis contributes only 183kg to the Aston's kerb weight – a figure we measured at 1590kg. It's clothed in a mixture of aluminium, steel, composite and magnesium body panels, and they all add up to a truly spectacular suit. The V8 Vantage is a surprisingly low, squat car, the proportions creating an aggressive aura even before the shape is considered. It's

QUICK FACTS

Model tested	V8 Vantage
Price	£79,995
On sale	November 2005
0–60mph	4.9sec
Top speed	175mph (claimed)
Economy	17.4mpg
Emissions	406g/km CO$_2$
70–0mph	47.6m
Skidpan	0.98g

ROAD TEST

22 NOVEMBER 2005

Volume 246

No 8 | 5666

110TH ANNIVERSARY ISSUE

AUTOCAR

CARS: THE FUTURE

60 EXTRA PAGES

KX55 KWR

ACCELERATION Standing qtr mile 13.5sec/107.8mph Standing km 24.4sec/139.7mph 30–70mph 4.2sec

30mph	40	50	60	70	80	90	100	110	120	130	140
1.9s	2.7s	3.8s	4.9s	6.1s	7.9s	9.4s	11.5s	13.8s	16.3s	20.1s	23.9s

0   5s   10s   15s   20s   25s   30s

DRY/WET BRAKING

30mph-0	30mph-0	Dry 50mph-0	Wet 50mph-0	70mph-0	70mph-0
8.5m	9.8m	23.8m	31.4m	47.6m	75.1m

0   10m   20m   30m   40m   50m   60m   70m

ACCELERATION IN GEAR

MPH	2nd	3rd	4th	5th	6th
20–40	2.5	3.6	4.9	7.5	7.7
30–50	2.3	3.3	4.5	7.3	7.3
40–60	2.2	3.1	4.3	7.2	6.9
50–70	2.3	3.0	4.1	7.0	6.5
60–80		3.1	4.0	6.7	6.2
70–90		3.2	4.1	6.8	6.2
80–100		3.4	4.4	6.9	6.3
90–110			4.8	6.9	6.4
100–120			5.6	7.4	6.9
110–130				7.9	
120–140				8.7	
130–150				10.3	

MAX SPEED IN GEAR

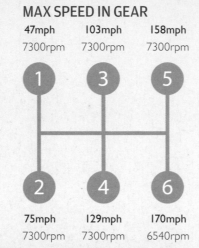

① 47mph	③ 103mph	⑤ 158mph
7300rpm	7300rpm	7300rpm

② 75mph	④ 129mph	⑥ 170mph
7300rpm	7300rpm	6540rpm

ECONOMY

	TEST		CLAIMED	
Average	17.4mpg	Urban	11.2mpg
Touring	21.9mpg	Ex-urb	22.6mpg
Track	7.6mpg	Comb	16.4mpg
Tank size	77 litres	Test range	294 miles

CABIN NOISE

Idle 57dbA **Max revs in 3rd** 87dbA **30mph** 61dbA **50mph** 67dbA **70mph** 73dbA

HEADLIGHTS

Dipped beam Okay **Full beam** Excellent

Test notes Decent range on full beam

WIPERS

Good coverage, but some noise

TESTER'S NOTES

The Vantage is an enjoyable and easy-going car on the GT circuit. It matches arch-rival 911's peak speed around the long left after turn 3, but steadily loses ground to its German rival just about everywhere else – under braking, through the corners and under acceleration – especially leaving the tight T5. However, the final time is admirably close. The Aston claws some time back through the tricky, cambered, crested, third gear esses of T2 – the 911 dislikes the repeated direction change at speed while the Aston calmly scythes through. On the wet circuit the Vantage was easily provoked into oversteer with the throttle, but the DSC would sort things out if switched on, albeit too late to help you with quick lap times.

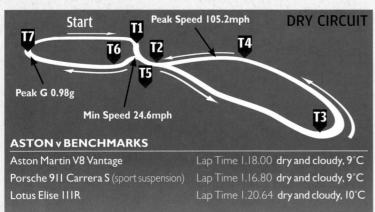

DRY CIRCUIT

Start
T7 T6 T1 T2 T5 T4
Peak Speed 105.2mph
Peak G 0.98g
Min Speed 24.6mph
T3

ASTON v BENCHMARKS

Aston Martin V8 Vantage	Lap Time 1.18.00	dry and cloudy, 9°C
Porsche 911 Carrera S (sport suspension)	Lap Time 1.16.80	dry and cloudy, 9°C
Lotus Elise 111R	Lap Time 1.20.64	dry and cloudy, 10°C

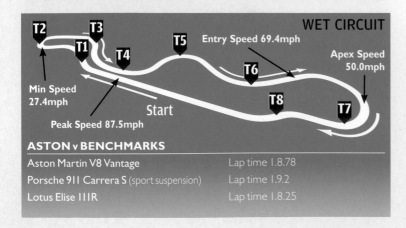

WET CIRCUIT

T2 T3 T1 T4 T5
Entry Speed 69.4mph
T6
Apex Speed 50.0mph
Min Speed 27.4mph
Start
Peak Speed 87.5mph
T8 T7

ASTON v BENCHMARKS

Aston Martin V8 Vantage	Lap time 1.8.78
Porsche 911 Carrera S (sport suspension)	Lap time 1.9.2
Lotus Elise 111R	Lap time 1.8.25

LATERAL G

Wet 0.76g Dry 0.98g

SLALOM

11.5s

0s   5s   10s

Respectable slalom, but wet g soundly beaten by 911 (0.83)

50mm shorter and 40mm lower than a Porsche 911
Carrera S, and considerably more compact than
big brother DB9: 313mm shorter, 60mm lower and
with a 140mm shorter wheelbase. These diminutive
dimensions give the V8 Vantage a real wheel-at-each-
corner stance.

At the front, the familiar Aston grille spreads out
into a bluff, wide-arched front with pronounced
wheelarches, before flowing tightly back into a
typically compact coupé form. It then bulges back
out with thick-set rear arches and a cut-off tail
under which nestle fat twin tailpipes. The details
are luxuriously effective: notice the intricate xenon
lights with inner LED indicators; the cut-out vents
struck through with a line of chrome that flows into
the metal of the door, and the elegant flip out door
handles. Even the door mirrors are unusual, with
slender supports attaching them to the body.

Under the muscled skin, the Vantage follows
current Aston thinking: forged aluminium double
wishbones are hung from the chassis with
conventional coil springs, tubular dampers and anti-
roll bars front and rear. The engine is at the front,

but mounted considerably back in the chassis, with
drive passing to the rear wheels via a carbon fibre
propshaft surrounded by a cast aluminium torque
tube. The six-speed manual gearbox – a Graziano
unit – is packaged at the rear along with the
limited-slip differential, aiding the excellent weight
distribution of 51:49 front to rear.

For the necessary under-bonnet fireworks, Aston
has turned to one of its PAG partners. The new
V8 is loosely based on the Jaguar unit first seen in
the mid-'90s and used in the S type, the XJ and the
XK. It's been radically overhauled, however, and for
Aston's purposes is built in Cologne alongside its V12.

The capacity of the all-alloy block has been
increased from 4.2 to 4.3 litres and now features
dry-sump lubrication to better withstand cornering
forces and allow it to be fitted lower in the chassis.
With a unique bore and stroke, the Aston V8 has
its own pistons, conrods and crankshaft, along with
its own head, manifolds and each of the 32 valves.
There's variable timing on the inlet camshaft, plus a
resonance induction system, and the spent gases are
expelled through a 4-2-1 manifold on each bank of

Central starter button glows red when you dip the clutch

Alloy pedals look good and are well spaced and weighted for heel-and-toe changes

Leather-wrapped wheel slabby in design and not as well-contoured to hold as we'd like

ABOVE Our test car had the basic grey dash – optional trims much more enticing.

OPPOSITE Traditional clock: one of many well thought-out details in a cabin that disguises its Ford Motor Company components very well; Aston logos embossed into aluminium sill kickplates.

cylinders and out of an exhaust system that features a bypass valve to boost noise above 4500rpm.

The results look compelling on paper: a 911-crushing 380bhp at a howling 7300rpm and 302lb ft of torque at 5000rpm, with the promise of 75 per cent of that from as low as 1500rpm. Stopping this British bruiser are 355mm discs at the front and 330mm discs at the rear.

PERFORMANCE AND DYNAMICS

Settle INTO the densely padded sports seat and twist the ignition key. The Vantage's dash lights up and you thumb the glowing red starter button to wake the V8. It explodes into life with a flamboyance to match the exterior styling before settling to a tug boat-like throbbing idle.

This isn't the tightly regulated, slightly synthetic vee-eight soundtrack of a German performance car, nor the mellifluous baritone of a Maserati GranSport, rather a more wholesome, old-fashioned V8 voice where you can almost hear each piston stroke. The trick exhaust appears to keep the flaps open from idle to around 2000rpm, so moving away and loping

along in this rev band is accompanied by a delicious, industrial muscle-car gurgle.

The raucous soundtrack doesn't mean that the V8 Vantage is crude, however: one of the strengths of this car is its easy-going nature around town and in traffic. Predictably, the engine will pull from next to nothing, but it's the ride quality that sets the Vantage apart from its rivals. It soaks up surface changes and irregularities with genuine talent – easily beating a 911 Carrera S for bump absorbtion.

Despite this apparent cosseting, the Vantage is nevertheless a car that you have to really drive. The gearlever moves around the gate with a sturdy, mechanical feel that often requires effort from the shoulder. The brakes require confident application of your toes – as does the clutch – and the steering has a weighted, oily feeling as the wheel turns in your palms. We suspect plenty of owners will value the constant reminder that they're driving something as special as an Aston Martin, but to most it will feel a bit much at times.

Up the pace and the ride quality that impresses so much at slower speeds tails away. It never crashes over ridges like a 911, but neither does it flow over apparently decent motorway surfaces with the same ease. Instead, there's a constant fidget beneath that takes the edge off the Vantage's cruising ability.

Still, the V8 has now warmed through, and it's time to get the rev needle working in a higher segment of its reverse arc. The raw, unabashed, shrieking fury that emerges from the tail-pipes above 4500rpm is just about consolidated by the accelerative force, but we emphasise the word 'just'. We equalled Aston's claim of 4.9sec for the 0–60mph sprint, and that feels about right from our impressions on the road, trailing the Carrera S by three tenths of a second and the 500bhp BMW M6 by two. By 100mph – attained in 11.5sec – the gap to the 911 has widened to seven tenths and the M6 (9.7sec) is rather rapidly disappearing up the road.

Perhaps more telling are the in-gear figures. When the Aston is wailing in its powerband, it's just about a match for the 911 – witness the 50–70mph time in third gear, just a tenth behind the German car. But accelerate over the same increment in fifth gear and the gap becomes almost a second (6.1 plays 5.2sec). The bottom line is this: the Vantage requires extending through the rev range if it's to feel top-drawer quick, and the throttle response and pick up low down doesn't have the same crisp and

SPECIFICATIONS V8 VANTAGE

DIMENSIONS

Front track 1568mm **Rear track** 1562mm **Width including mirrors** 2022m **Width excluding mirrors** 1866mm **Front interior width** 1385mm

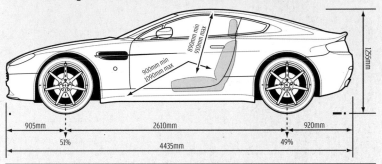

ENGINE

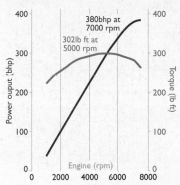

Red line	7300rpm
Power	380bhp at 7000rpm
Torque	302lb ft at 5000rpm
Type/fuel	V8, 4300cc/petrol
Made of/Installation	Alloy/front, longitudinal, rwd
Power to weight	242bhp per tonne*
Torque to weight	192lb ft per tonne*
Specific output	88bhp per litre
Compression ratio	11.3:1
Bore/stroke	89.0/86.0mm
Valve gear	4 per cyl, DOHC per bank

TRANSMISSION

Gearbox 6-speed manual
Ratios/mph per 1000rpm
Final drive ratio 3.91

1st 3.15/6.4	2nd 1.97/10.3
3rd 1.44/14.1	4th 1.15/17.6
5th 0.94/21.6	6th 0.78/26.0

CHASSIS AND BODY

Construction	Bonded aluminium structure
Weight/as tested	1570kg/1590.5kg
Drag coefficient	0.34
Wheels	Alloy (f) 8.5Jx19, (r) 9.5Jx19
Tyres	235/45 ZR19, 275/40 ZR19 Bridgestone Potenza
Spare	Mousse

STEERING

Type Hydraulically-assisted rack and pinion
Turns lock-to-lock 3.1
Turning circle 11.1m

SUSPENSION

Front Double wishbones, coil springs, anti-roll bar
Rear Double wishbones, coil springs, anti-roll bar

BRAKES

Front 355mm ventilated discs
Rear 330mm ventilated discs
Anti-lock Standard, with EBD
Parking brake Hand operated

THE SMALL PRINT *Power- and torque-to-weight figures calculated using manufacturer's claimed kerb weight © Autocar 2005. Test results may not be reproduced without editor's written permission. For information on the V8 Vantage contact Aston Martin, Banbury Road, Gaydon, Warwickshire CV35 0DB, 01926 644300, www.www.astonmartin.com. Cost-per-mile figures calculated over three years/36,000 miles, including depreciation and maintenance but not insurance; Lloyds TSB Autolease (0870 600 6333). Insurance quote covers 35-year-old professional male with clean licence and full no-claims bonus living in Swindon; from What Car? Insurance (0845 123 2618). Contract hire figure based on a three-year lease/36,000-mile contract including maintenance; from Lombard (0870 902 3311).

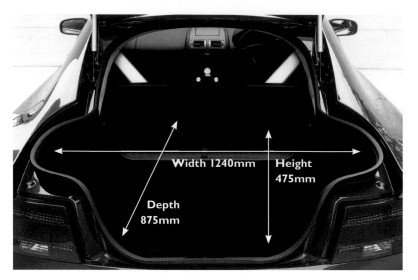

Width 1240mm

Height 475mm

Depth 875mm

car's vague modulation, the Vantage's stoppers can really be leant on with reassurance once you're used to them. Even during five hard laps of our GT circuit they resisted fade to a level we would never have predicted.

Less impressive is the anti-lock unit on slippery roads: despite a higher kerb weight the Aston nearly matches the 911 when braking from 70mph in the dry (47.6m v 44m) but it needs over 11 metres more when the surface is wet. The pedal suddenly becomes hard underfoot – as if you've trodden on packed snow – although the car's directional stability is without question.

Initially, as the speeds rise, the Vantage feels like a sizeable chunk of English craftsmanship to thread along a challenging road; a sensation heightened by the low, far back driving position. But a rapid acclimatisation process is aided by some core Vantage strengths. The steering has well-judged weight, accuracy and a fair amount of feel, and there is a surprising level of body control at speed. Despite the Vantage's size and weight, you never get the feeling that the dampers will surrender and allow the elegant nose to hit the road through a compression.

ABOVE 300-litre boot above average for the class.

OPPOSITE 4.3-litre engine loosely based on Jaguar's 4.2-litre motor.

urgent response as a 911's. Dismiss for a moment the Aston's sound effects and you'll find that final layer of polish, of endlessly honed precision engineering, doesn't stand comparison with the Porsche.

Hauling the V8 down from such speeds is no great drama as the grooved discs prove more than up to the task. The initial hard pedal resistance reminds us of the DB9's brakes, but unlike that

INSTANT GROUP TEST EUROPE'S FINEST GTs SLUG IT OUT

MAKE	ASTON MARTIN 	BMW 	MASERATI 	PORSCHE
Model	V8	M6	GranSport	911 Carrera S
Price	£79,950	£80,755	£66,600	£65,000
Power	380bhp at 7000rpm	500bhp at 7750rpm	395bhp at 7000rpm	350bhp at 6600rpm
Torque	302lb ft at 5000rpm	384lb ft at 6100rpm	333lb ft at 4500rpm	295lb ft at 4600rpm
0–60mph	4.8sec	4.6sec	4.9sec	4.6sec
Top speed	175mph	155mph (limited)	180mph	182mph
Fuel consumption	16.2mpg	14.8mpg	15.2mpg	20.9mpg
Kerbweight	1570kg	1785kg	1672kg	1420kg
Boot space	300 litres	450 litres	315 litres	135 litres
CO_2/tax band	406g/km / 35 per cent	357g/km / 35 per cent	434g/km / 35 per cent	227g/km / 35 per cent
We think	Charismatic British GT has fantastic visual and aural drama. So nearly there, but lacks polish of the Porsche.	Has more soul – and more performance – than you'd ever imagine. Only useless range and so-so brakes let it down.	The left-field choice. Strong and characterful engine, but would struggle to keep up on a wet road.	One of the great sports cars. Brilliant chassis, goes almost as well as M6, and stops better, for £16k less.
VERDICT	★★★★	★★★★⯪	★★★⯪	★★★★★

This production car has a better-balanced chassis than the early examples we drove, which seemed to have a delay between the inputs given at the helm and the eventual behaviour of the rear axle. Those early cars felt like they were made from two slightly different halves, and drivers found themselves sawing at the wheel through a corner, trying to make sense of what was going on underneath them.

With that sensation removed – perhaps thanks to improved build tolerances on this production example – the Vantage is a forgiving and sympathetic car to drive. It grips well when required, and slips into understeer as the limit approaches before adopting a tail-out stance. At this point, a stab of throttle will keep the car sliding in a progressive and entertaining manner – although you'll need a fair few revs on the dial if you're to have accurate control of the slide. If the road surface is slippery, it will readily oversteer with the DSC off, but as our wet circuit experience proved, when driven in such a manner, it's easier to control than a 911.

Nevertheless, in most areas, there's no escaping the fact that the 911 has the edge. Not just in acceleration and outright grip, but also in those finer

WHAT IT COSTS

ASTON MARTIN V8 VANTAGE		Airbags front/side	■/■
On-the-road price	£79,995	Curtain airbags	na
Price as tested	£83,525	Sports exhaust	na
Retained value 3yrs	na	ESP and traction control	■
Typical PCP pcm	na	Integrated telephone	£795
Contract hire pcm	na	Electrically asjustable seats	■
Cost per mile	na	Metallic paint	■
CO2	406g/km	**Satellite navigation**	**£1750**
Tax at 22/40% pcm	£512/£931	Tyre pressure sensors	■
Insurance/typical quote	20/£809	Tracker system	£795
		Alarm upgrade	**£195**
EQUIPMENT CHECKLIST		Trip computer	■
Steering reach adjust	■	Parking sensors	■
19in alloys	**£995**	Cruise control	£295
Auto climate control	■	Xenon headlamps	£495
Automatic lights and wipers	na/na	6-CD autochanger	■
Powerfold mirrors	**£295**	Heated front seats	£295
Adjustable dampers	na		
Monotone leather trim	**£695**		
Duotone leather trim	£1195	Options in **bold** fitted to test car
Heated front screen	**£295**	■ = Standard na = not available

TEST SCORECARD

ENGINE ★★★☆
Revs enthusiastically once into its stride, but response isn't that sharp lower down the rev range. Could do with a bit more power.

TRANSMISSION ★★★★
Gearshift is rewarding to get right, but can feel like too much effort when you're not in the mood. Hooking reverse is a cumbersome task.

STEERING ★★★★
Well-judged power steering is progressive moving from straight-ahead and accurate once on lock. Feel is reasonable.

BRAKES ★★★★
Weighty response to an initial application, but nicely graded when you work them harder. They resist fade admirably.

HANDLING ★★★★
The Vantage drives like a classical GT car: nicely balanced and with a natural tendency to oversteer when provoked. Fair grip levels.

RIDE ★★★☆
Impressive low speed ride around town let down by a motorway ride that never truly settles.

ECONOMY ★★☆
Not as efficient as a 911, much better than an M6. With a decent tank size of 77 litres, the touring range is a respectable 300 miles.

DRIVING POSITION ★★★★
A proper laid back driving position and good ergonomics create the right atmosphere and make the V8 comfortable. Adequate visibility.

CONTROLS ★★★☆
Overall, they look better than they actually work. Which isn't to say they're bad, just that items like the sat-nav control could be better.

EQUIPMENT ★★★☆
Most of the basics are here, but you have to pay extra for full leather trim and sat-nav, which seems steep for an £80,000 car.

LIVEABILITY ★★★★
Cabin is roomy, shelf behind seats useful, and the boot can swallow a surprising amount of luggage.

QUALITY ★★★
Fit and finish is impressive, some of the creaks less so. Doesn't have the sense of solidity of its German rivals.

VALUE ★★★
You pay for style, as the performance is available elsewhere for less. Should hold onto its value tenaciously, however.

SAFETY ★★★★
A bonded aluminium sandwich construction should be strong, and there's a fair airbag count. Traction control is standard.

TRACKWORK ★★★★
For a fairly heavy GT car the Aston turns in a good performance. Brakes resist fade, and there's enough grip.

DESIRABILITY ★★★★★
Probably the Vantage's trump card. Looks stunning from all angles, and gets a great reaction wherever it goes.

NOISE ★★★★★
Deep and menacing V8 rumbling at low revs and a piercing howl above 4500rpm.

traits: quality of steering, outright control and agility. The build up of power assistance and self-centring of the Aston's steering rack is more obvious, and occasionally it kicks back through the column. It doesn't have quite the same iron-fisted control over a challenging road as a 911 – occasionally squirming at the rear over undulating surfaces or as you put down full power, and it can't change direction with comparable speed and precision.

LIVING WITH IT

The question any potential V8 Vantage buyer should ask themselves is this: how would they feel to wake up in the morning, look out of the window and spy the Vantage on the drive. The answer, we're certain, is 'pretty good, thank you'.

The good news is that there are more reasons than this alone to buy a V8 Vantage. The dashboard is a mix of first class aesthetics and ease of use. Elsewhere, the cabin works well: the seats are comfortable for long journeys and drop low in the car, although their lateral support can't match

AUTOCAR VERDICT

For many, the sight and sound of this car will be enough to fire a desire that overwhelms objective considerations. But perhaps we shouldn't be so surprised that the V8 Vantage isn't quite accomplished enough to topple its established opposition. Porsche has been building 911s for more than 40 years. This Aston, on the other hand, is built on cutting-edge body technology with which its maker has only four years' experience, in a factory that is two years old, using a workforce that has grown by 50 per cent in the past three years.

The V8 is very capable, but it's short of that final, magical polish that separates a good car from a great one — the polish that comes from endless refinement. Its performance is strong enough, and its dynamic repertoire, while no threat to the 911's, is broad. Where it really scores is with its looks and classy aura. If that's enough to tempt you, we wouldn't argue.

Nearly as able as it is hugely desirable ★★★★

This means you can expect around 300 miles from a tankful when cruising — far better than that offered by the gas-guzzling BMW.

Perhaps the most important — and hardest to judge — measure of the Aston's everyday usability is its mechanical integrity. We've driven a selection of V8 Vantages now, and although the standard of fit and finish is impressive, the cars lack the deep-rooted feeling of engineering togetherness that a Porsche or BMW exudes.

LEFT V8 Vantage's pace not quite as rapid as the phenomenal soundtrack suggests.

BELOW Cabin has great sense of occasion; optional trims enhance it further.

those in a Carrera. Behind the seats there's a useful carpeted storage area — big enough for a briefcase — complete with evocative aluminium roll-over spars.

The Vantage is a hatchback, and the 300-litre boot under the parcel shelf is well-shaped and large for the class. The interior of our road test car was in rather conservative shades, but there are more vibrant, appealing options available, such as bamboo wood or aluminium. But these will cost you dear: full leather trim is extra, as is satellite navigation and the gorgeous, thin-spoke 19in wheels. Next to the full-house specification of the M6, the Vantage's looks a little stingy, and it will be easy for prospective owners to rapidly inflate the cost of their cars.

Still, the extra initial outlay should be more than offset by admirable residual value performance. There is currently a substantial waiting list for the Vantage and any owners at the front of the queue will no doubt make money should they sell their car on within a few months. If they choose to keep it, they can expect thirst somewhere between that of an M6 and a 911: we achieved 17.4mpg as an average.

FANTASTIC FOUR

RAPIDE CONCEPT The most fantastic thing about this four-door Aston Martin Rapide concept isn't the way it looks, it's the way it drives. Steve Cropley was first behind the wheel

If you first set eyes on Aston Martin's remarkable Rapide directly from behind – as I did – you'll find there's almost no clue to the fact that the car has four doors. It's so low, and its lines are so sleek and balanced as they undulate away from you towards the low nose, that you imagine at first that this is some new breed of Aston two-door. As if they needed another of those...

Not until you move to the side of the car does it even cross your mind that this mighty coupé actually has two decent-sized doors let into each side, providing access to a low-slung but surprisingly roomy cabin. Your shock is followed immediately by admiration. According to Aston's recently appointed design director, Marek Reichman, his designers were briefed to make 'the most beautiful four-door car in the world' and here, before your eyes, is arguable proof that they've succeeded.

'The proportions of this car had to be perfect', says Aston's dynamic chairman and CEO, Dr Ulrich Bez, instigator of the project, 'otherwise we wouldn't have built it.'

The Rapide is a full 30cm (12in) longer than the DB9, already a big car, and only four centimetres (1.5in) taller. At a full five metres in overall length, it is about the same as a standard BMW 7-series, yet it is an amazing 13cm (6in) lower (and also 4cm wider). Any car designer will tell you how difficult it is to give such a long, low structure a look of balance and practicality – especially when you've got to cope with an exaggerated windscreen rake and position two doors along the sides – yet there's no sign of stretch in the Rapide, just a sense of grace and harmony, and an awe-inspiring sense of scale.

'We've avoided giving this car a wedge shape,' says Reichman. 'If the two-door Astons are like athletes on the starting blocks, the Rapide is the athlete in full flight.'

The Rapide project was born just six months ago, as part of a telephone conversation between Bez, who was in Warwickshire, and Reichman, who at the

FIRST DRIVE

10 JANUARY 2006

Volume 247

No 2 | 5672

ABOVE Sleek styling effortlessly blends rear doors into graceful coupé-like body.

time was designing Ford interiors in Detroit. Bez was offering Reichman the Aston design director's job and, as well as demanding his new design boss start at a fortnight's notice, Bez also spelled out his plan to put a working four-door Aston concept car on the marque's Detroit show stand. By the time Reichman arrived for work, he'd already done a lot of Aston homework and was armed with a bulging book full of fresh sketches.

All of which is why, a few days before Christmas, we were standing in a quietly freezing corner of the Premier Automotive Group's vast test track at Gaydon not just to view the world's one-and-only Aston Martin Rapide, but also to drive it. Driving is not usually an exercise associated with new concept cars. They ordinarily appear as highly attractive lumps of plastic and clay, only occasionally acquiring the ability to be driven some months after debut.

This Rapide, however, breaks the rules. The car behind whose wheel I was about to slip, and which is currently on display at the Detroit motor show, is a full-performance V12-powered saloon. The concept car is closely related, mechanically speaking, to the showroom version Aston Martin could build at a rate of around 500 a year and launch in 2008, priced around £160,000 of today's money. That would

trump Porsche's forthcoming Panamera four-door by a clear year.

Bez is an old Porsche employee and watches carefully what it does, but he denies that Porsche's plans have any bearing on Aston's strategy, or that a launch date for the Rapide has been chosen. 'We don't need it yet,' he says. 'We have our other models to establish in the market. There is still a strong waiting list for the DB9, the V8 Vantage is only a few months old and we have made more Vanquishes than we ever planned.'

The other thing Bez says he doesn't need at present is the Lagonda marque, especially now it has donated the name of its big Rapide saloon (55 of which were made between 1961 and 1965) to the new project. Modern Lagondas might make an appearance at some time in the future, Bez says, for projects that don't sit correctly under the Aston umbrella, but Aston people simply haven't done any thinking in that direction yet. Part of the Rapide's job is to show how easily the Aston Martin brand extends to a full-size sporting saloon, and how the versatile VH platform — already used for the 911-chasing V8 Vantage and the Le Mans-racing DBR9 GT — can also work in a car whose comfort and refinement will be an even greater priority.

FAST, FABULOUS FOUR-DOORS CARS THAT INSPIRED THE RAPIDE

1939 Aston Martin Atom prototype was made just before WW2 started.

1970s AM Lagonda prototype, based on DBS. Only seven were made.

Early 1990s Porsche 989 concept won much approval but was canned.

Lagonda Vignale: exquisite four-door 1993 concept car that was never made.

BASICALLY RIGHT

For driving, the Rapide's basic ingredients seem highly encouraging. The chassis and suspension are very closely related to those well-proven in the DB9, except that the extruded aluminium platform is lengthened by 25 centimetres to provide extra rear space, a move Aston engineers are positive won't interfere with the four-door's overall rigidity. The car has carbon brakes and calipers, Aston Martin's first use of them, and they should provide huge stopping power since the Rapide weighs only 140 kilograms more than a DB9.

Under the bonnet was Aston's 6.0-litre V12 with its power output gently lifted to 480bhp (from 450), driving through the same ZF Touchtronic gearbox as in the DB9, complete with paddle-shift.

ON THE INSIDE

The driver's door is the same butterfly affair as a DB9's, opening 12 degrees upwards to clear kerbs and obstacles. It opens wide, but there's a fair-sized sill to step over before you slide into the deeply shaped bucket, below the low roof. There's plenty

BELOW LEFT
Rear doors are small, especially the glass, but access to back is good; decent boot space easily accessed through hatch.

BELOW Rapide amazingly complete for a concept: it's like a production car to drive.

of legroom and headroom, and no sense of a driving position compromised to enhance the rear room. The cabin decor – wood, aluminium and grained leather – is recognisable from the DB9, but Aston Martin can offer so many variations of colour and trim that variety is easy to provide. The instrument pack is Aston's usual display of watch-like quality, and there's an impressive analogue clock in mid-dash by Jaeger-LeCoultre, the Swiss firm which provided instruments for Astons as long ago as 1929.

Dominating the entire interior is the light which streams in through the see-through polycarbonate roof, whose view-the-clouds quality can be turned opaque with a switch, but which allows light to flood in anyway. It's one of those features which, once you've sampled it, you know all cars need. Prominent on the dash is Aston's big glass starter button, flanked by push-buttons to control the six-speed transmission. With a foot on the brake you turn the key then thumb the glowing button. There's a second of seamless whirring, then a slightly remote bark as the V12 bursts into life. Nothing buzzes or rattles; there isn't a sign of the usual hot-rod nature of prototypes. Amazingly, this first Aston Rapide could be a production car.

Foot still on brake, you press the D button. Foot off the brake, onto the gas and the car glides away; glides away a bit too fast, actually, given that this is your first five yards in the car and its creators are standing right there, watching you mess with their pride and job. But the accelerator is lighter than expected, and there's no shortage of poke. Before we've gone half a mile, it's apparent that this will be an extremely fast car, no less quick (to anything but the stopwatch) than a DB9. That means a 0–60mph sprint time usefully below five seconds and a top speed somewhere north of 180mph. It may even be that the Rapide has better aerodynamics (and possibly even better cruising fuel consumption) than its siblings, given its extra length and probable better drag factor (Cd). All action is accompanied by an aristocratic V12 growl, most of it from the rear. Mechanical noise is hardly heard.

Three things stand out: visibility, manoeuvrability and ride comfort. It is amazing how well you can see out of this car, especially in tight corners when thick, steeply angled windscreen pillars usually get in the way. But the pillars are neatly angled for minimum intrusion and there's a new mounting system for the mirrors which allows you to see clearly through the quarter-windows above them. This, and all that ethereal light from above, set about reducing the apparent size of this big car.

THE DESIGNER REICHMAN FOR THE JOB

Marek Reichman has been looking forward to 2006 more than most years because he can start talking to his car designer friends again, now that the Rapide, his night-and-day project for six months, has broken cover. For half a year he has had to avoid conversations with his peers for fear of letting the Rapide cat out of the bag. 'Even if you say, "Oh nothing much," when someone asks you about your first project at Aston, you're still in danger of giving off vibes,' he says. 'You're better off saying nothing at all.'

Reichman has had a dream career since graduating from the Royal College of Art in 1991. He was sponsored there by Land Rover, and worked for it until BMW acquired the Rover Group, whereupon he was transferred to its Designworks studio in California. There he came up with the face of the latest Range Rover. After five years he returned to the UK, working with the team that designed the Rolls-Royce Phantom, before taking off to Dearborn to work on Lincoln and Ford projects. He was designing interiors for a new range of Fords when he took a call from Ulrich Bez at Aston Martin, who offered him the design boss's job and mentioned a four-door project. The rest is history.

Designer Reichman: has been living and breathing Rapide for six months.

The impression continues when you drive the car with a bit more energy through tight curves. The steering gearing is the same as the DB9's at present, and because of the foot of extra wheelbase there's a feeling it could be sharper (it will be, says Bez, whom I accompanied on his very first drive of the car). But the whole thing is light to steer and easy to manoeuvre. There's no sense that the Rapide will be daunting to drive. However, I have highest hope of all for the ride, which is certain to be enhanced over a DB9's by the extra foot of wheelbase. The part of the Gaydon track we used had precious few testing bumps, but the car's flatness in corners, the apparently excellent damper control and the way the widened track contains body roll virtually as well as an Aston coupé, makes it clear this will be a great road car.

Our time with the Rapide was brief, but before leaving I had one thing to do: get in the back. Bez makes no claim that the Rapide's rear is spacious, but I was encouraged that the rear seats might suit the fuller figure when 6ft 4in Reichman planted himself in there to please the photographer. Sure enough, I fitted too. Not comfortably enough for a trip to the south of France, but quite well enough to have travelled 100 miles in there. Legroom was the main issue: the car has very comfortable seats and plenty of headroom. People of smaller stature will find the Rapide snug and practical, so much so that they will have a hard time believing this Aston Martin Rapide is a strong candidate for the world's quickest saloon, if not in a straight line, then certainly point-to-point. That's a heck of a thing to be able to say about a one-off.

OPPOSITE Dashboard largely borrowed from DB9, though centre console gets new silver finish; paddle-shift auto gearbox.

FAR LEFT Boot has concealed bubbly storage. Cheers; headlights beautifully detailed and highly effective.

BELOW Smooth shape instantly recognisable as an Aston: rear doors well-integrated into fastback shape.

ASTON ROAD TRIP

PRODRIVE V8 VANTAGE It's 100 years since the Isle of Man TT road race was first held. Colin Goodwin celebrates with a pilgrimage to the Meccas of UK road racing in Prodrive's Aston V8 Vantage

What an amazing coincidence. We booked this Prodrive-tweaked Aston Martin V8 Vantage ages ago, yet on the very day that we collect it from Prodrive's Banbury factory, David Richards is at Aston's Gaydon HQ announcing to the world that he and a few minted associates have purchased the company. He is due to make the announcement at a press conference at 1pm. I've just passed the Gaydon exit on the M40, and since it's 12.45pm, Richards must be warming up for his moment at the mike.

This hack, who would rather be on the road in a fast car than at a press conference, is heading north at a brisk clip with a stack of CDs and Twixes on the passenger seat. The destination is Stranraer, Scotland, where I am catching the fast ferry to Belfast to hook up with our snapper Stan Papior.

Tomorrow we are meeting up with Robert Dunlop, brother of legendary bike racer Joey, who will show us the finer points of the seven-mile Dundrod road course that's used for the Ulster Grand Prix bike race, and which formed part of the course used for the Tourist Trophy car race in the 1950s. The day after that we're travelling to the Isle of Man for a lap around the TT course with a bloke who has been around it at an average speed of 124mph. This year marks the centenary of the TT races and I'm always looking for an excuse to drive around the course. I have done so on several occasions, but never in a machine as potent as this Aston.

I had a very quick go in the prototype Prodrive Aston with David Richards when I spent a day shadowing him last year. It has a power boost to 425bhp (up from 380bhp), reworked suspension and a more vocal exhaust system. Special wheels, too, and a carbon fibre rear spoiler that, together with a carbon front lip, reduces lift by 45 per cent. Unfortunately, it also makes the car look a bit pikey to my eyes.

The suspension features electronically adjustable damping that can be switched from the standard setting to a sports setting for fast road and track

FEATURE

11 APRIL 2007

Volume 252

No 2 I 5736

ROBERT DUNLOP MASTER OF ROAD RACING

At the TT, riders are set off at intervals and race against the clock, but at the Ulster GP they set off all in one go just like a normal race. And that is the only part of the event about which you can use the word 'normal'. From the grandstand we arrive at Rushey Hill and a section called the Flying Kilo. "A superbike will hit around 190mph along here," says Robert Dunlop. He has to be kidding. The road is not particularly wide and it certainly isn't smooth. Just holding on must be challenging enough. Soon you hit a junction with the main road that runs between the airport and the city. The road is dead straight as it drops into a valley and then rises up the other side. Again, the bikes are up over 160mph before knocking down a gear for Deer's Leap, a blind crest that's also a corner. "It's a 140mph corner," reports Dunlop, "and you get a big wheelie on the exit." We then turn right off the main road and go up what is no more than a country lane. Trees overhang and Dunlop advises that you have to watch out for damp patches.

"This is Budore. My son William crashed here and went straight through that hedge and into a field." Both Dunlop's sons race on the roads and both are quick. Dunlop's face tightens when I ask him if it's nerve-wracking watching his boys race. Last year a superbike averaged over 130mph around here: madness.

driving. The exhaust is switchable to quiet, auto and to a sport setting in which the exhaust valve is permanently open. Prodrive says that is for when "conditions allow", which is short for "when the old bill isn't about".

Several hours later, the whole world knows about Aston's sale and I am turning off the M6 north of Carlisle and hammering along the A75 towards Dumfries and Stranraer. When you get to Carlisle, you think you're nearly to Stranraer, but you're not, because it's 100 miles to the west. There are no cameras on the A75, which is good because this Aston does not hang around. It sounds fantastic with the volume set to loud. The stiffest suspension setting is unnecessarily harsh for the public road, and I'd save myself £5581 and leave it off the order form. The £3995 wheels save 9kg, so they can stay. Deleting the aero pack saves another £2937, so that just leaves £6239 for the motor and exhaust mods. The standard V8 isn't slow, but with an extra 45bhp the Prodrive car rips along.

DUNDROD CIRCUIT

Track distance 7.29 miles **Lap record** 3m 23.655s (130.829mph) **Who by** Ian Hutchinson, Kawasaki ZX-10R, 2006

The folk at Stena line are obviously of the "you can't have too much grunt" persuasion, too. They've fitted their fast ferry with two General Electric gas turbines, as used on Boeing 747s and two smaller units used on Saab's Grippen fighter. Flat out she'll do over 40 knots, so in a couple of hours I'm at our Belfast hotel.

It's a lovely morning as Stan and I leave the hotel. This city is certainly on the up. We drive past the Harland and Wolff shipyard. The company still carries out refits and maintenance but the place looks abandoned. Hard to believe that once the Titanic, Canberra and other great vessels were built here and that through its gates walked thousands of workers.

But if the stillness of the shipyards is depressing, a drive into Belfast city is not. We drive slowly along the Falls Road reading the graffiti as we go. The Falls Road – a name so often heard on the news when I was growing up. This is part of the history of my generation. Today, in the bright sun, the Falls Road seems peaceful. You can take a tour and be shown

a Bobby Sands hunger strike mural and other landmarks, but for me it is enough to see people leading normal lives again.

Dundrod is no more than 20 minutes out of Belfast, on the road to the international airport. We find the village easily, but have to ask a local for directions to the grandstand and to the circuit's start line. A white four-door E36 3-series is parked opposite the grandstand. Sitting inside, with a fag on the go, is Robert Dunlop.

Though 47-year-old Robert's career didn't match his brother's, he's won five TTs and numerous road races in Northern Ireland. He's still racing today, but only on 125cc bikes. The reason why is obvious when I shake hands with Dunlop, as he has only just enough power in his right hand to shake mine. At the 1994 Isle of Man TT the rear wheel of his Honda RC45 collapsed as he landed after the jump at Ballagh Bridge. His body was badly smashed, especially his right leg and right arm. Massive tendon damage to the latter has meant that he

ABOVE Robert Dunlop puts the Aston through its paces around the Dundrod road circuit.

INSET Reminders of The Troubles are everywhere in Belfast; fortunately they're just memories now.

ABOVE Isle of Man's roads are tight, bumpy and twisty. Great in the Aston, must be scary at 190mph on a superbike...

OPPOSITE What a view to accompany your fry-up; the Prodrive Aston drew plenty of other admiring glances during our road trip, too.

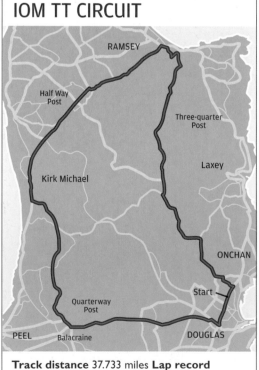

IOM TT CIRCUIT

RAMSEY

Half Way Post

Three-quarter Post

Laxey

Kirk Michael

ONCHAN

Start

Quarterway Post

PEEL

Balacraine

DOUGLAS

Track distance 37.733 miles **Lap record** 17m 29.26s (129.45mph) **Who by** John McGuinness, Honda Fireblade, 2006

is no longer able to wrestle a superbike on physically demanding road courses.

Dunlop drives the Aston beautifully and is extremely articulate. His entry in *Wikipedia* describes him as the world's toughest man. I wouldn't argue. He's fairly short in stature but massive in guts.

What I haven't told Stan is that our boat to Douglas on the Isle of Man doesn't leave Heysham until 2.15am, which is not too convenient as our ferry gets into Stranraer at 7pm and it doesn't take long to get to Heysham in a car as fast as the Vantage.

We arrive in Douglas at 6.15am and take the opportunity of quiet roads to knock off a quick lap of the 37.75-mile TT course. At lunchtime we're meeting up with Richard Quayle, known to bike fans as Milky, due to his resemblance to the Milky Bar Kid. Quayle is only the third Manxman to have won a TT, but had a terrifying crash in the 2003 races that prompted his retirement.

There are no speed limits outside of towns on the island, but that doesn't mean you can't be busted for irresponsible driving. The weather is perfect, which it often isn't. From Waterworks corner, just a few miles outside Ramsey, we have a fantastic view out across the Irish Sea. It is quite beautiful, with

MILKY QUAYLE THE 140MPH SURVIVOR

A few miles past Milky Quayle's house at Greeba Bridge is Ballacraine. It's a crossroads where the TT course turns right at the lights. Nothing complicated here. The riders accelerate away from the crossroads, flanked on either side by hedges and trees.

After winning in 2002, Quayle thought it would all come good for the following year. "I thought I'd earn some money in 2003," he says, "but as the TT approached I didn't even have any bikes. Then virtually at the last minute I sorted some machines. The Kawasaki superbike handled dreadfully at high speed, weaving around at almost 200mph. In the end we discovered it was an aerodynamic problem and that raising the rear by 25mm sorted it.

"The trouble was that this fix made the bike turn in extremely quickly. Just after Ballacraine I steered too close to a stone wall because I wasn't used to the quick steering. My shoulder hit the wall and I was pulled backwards, losing my grip on the handlebars."

Out of control, Quayle hit the other wall at 140mph and was pitched off the somersaulting bike. All his left ribs were broken, his spleen was removed and almost a kidney. Thankfully, he's now fully recovered.

I have been driven by plenty of great talents, but few passenger rides have been as interesting as the guided tour Quayle gives me around the TT course. His knowledge is incredible and he drives superbly. We drive through the village of Kirkmichael, where the road winds between houses. Unbelievably, the quick riders are doing 170mph here. The lap record for the TT course stands at over 129mph. How do these blokes do it?

Snaefell behind us, for once not shrouded in fog.

Milky Quayle lives in a converted chapel at Greeba. Walk out of his gate and you're on the TT course. "There are only two things I've ever wanted in life," says Quayle. "To race at the TT and to have a family." Trophies dotted around the house in cabinets and a mess of toys on the floor prove that life turned out all right for him.

Quayle's knowledge of the circuit is incredible. He knows every inch of kerb and every corner in minute detail.

Still the Aston is running perfectly and attracting a lot of attention. There's a constant stream of admirers as we line up to take the evening boat at Douglas back to Heysham. Four hours later we're back on the mainland and aiming back down the M6 for the journey to Prodrive at Banbury.

This is without question the best Aston Martin I've ever driven, including the Vanquish. With these Prodrive mods and a manual gearbox, I'd have it over the Jag XKR if I had the extra potatoes required. Fantastic. Over 1000 miles and not a single glitch. Richards will be chuffed. I'm looking forward to seeing what he does with Aston Martin.

ASTON V8 ROADSTER

V8 VANTAGE ROADSTER After a year-and-a-half wait since the launch of the V8 Vantage coupé, we find out whether our excitement over the arrival of a convertible version was justified

When a car sounds as good as the Aston Martin V8 Vantage coupé, the arrival of a convertible version is something that we are genetically obliged to get excited about. That we've had to wait a year and a half since the introduction of the coupé in 2005 hasn't dampened our enthusiasm one bit. And despite the apparent wait, the roadster has actually been on the cards since the inception of the V8 Vantage, which, when total production numbers soon exceed those of the DB7, will become Aston's most successful car ever. Rightly so. In our November 2005 road test we said we could understand entirely if you chose a V8 Vantage over a Porsche 911. Question is, does the roadster have all the desirability of the coupé?

DESIGN AND ENGINEERING ★★★★

Like the V8 Vantage coupé, the roadster is constructed on Aston Martin's VH (vertical-horizontal) platform, first seen on the Vanquish. Similar in principle to the basis of the Lotus Elise, the VH platform uses aluminium extrusions and castings, bonded and riveted together. This is both light (the chassis weighs just 197kg) and particularly well suited to convertible cars, with the majority of the car's rigidity coming from the chassis rather than exterior body panels. That said, for the roadster Aston has

QUICK FACTS

Model tested	V8 Vantage roadster 6-speed manual
Price	£91,000
Power	380bhp
Torque	302lb ft
0–60mph	5.2sec
Fuel economy	17.5mpg
CO_2 emissions	358g/km
70–0mph	44.6m
Skidpan	0.97g

ROAD TEST

25 APRIL 2007

Volume 252

No 4 I 5738

ROAD TEST ASTON MARTIN V8 VANTAGE ROADSTER

ACCELERATION Dry track, 17°C. Odometer reading 1367miles

30mph	40	50	60 70	80	90	100	110	120	130	140
2.2s	3.0s	4.0s	5.2s 5.8s	8.3s	10.0s	12.0s	14.6s	17.4s	21.6s	26.1s

0   5s   10s   15s   20s   25s

DRY/WET BRAKING 60–0mph 3.1sec

30mph-0	30mph-0			50mph-0	50mph-0			Dry 70mph-0		Wet 70mph-0
8.4m	9.4m			22.7m	26.0m			44.6m		52.7m

0   10m   20m   30m   40m   50m

ACCELERATION IN GEAR

MPH	2nd	3rd	4th	5th	6th
20–40	2.5	3.7	4.9	-	-
30–50	2.3	3.4	4.5	5.9	8.1
40–60	2.3	3.2	4.3	5.7	7.8
50–70	2.3	3.1	4.1	5.6	7.9
60–80	-	3.1	4.1	5.5	7.8
70–90	-	3.2	4.1	5.6	8.0
80–100	-	3.5	4.3	5.8	8.2
90–110	-	-	4.5	6.1	8.3
100–120	-	-	5.0	6.6	8.9
110–130	-	-	-	-	-
120–140	-	-	-	-	-

MAX SPEED IN GEAR

49mph	107mph	163mph
7300rpm	7300rpm	7300rpm

① ③ ⑤

② ④ ⑥

78mph	134mph	175mph
7300rpm	7300rpm	6490rpm

ECONOMY

	TEST		CLAIMED	
Average	17.5mpg		Urban	12.6mpg
Touring	22.1mpg		Ex-urb	26.6mpg
Track	6.8mpg		Comb	18.8mpg
Tank size	80 litres		Test range	308 miles

CABIN NOISE
Idle 57bA **Max revs in 3rd** 87bA **30mph** 61bA
50mph 69bA **70mph** 75bA

SAFETY
Dynamic stability and traction control; driver, passenger and side airbags; pre-tensioning seatbelts, pop-up roll bars
EuroNCAP crash rating na
Pedestrian rating na

GREEN RATING
CO_2 emissions 358g/km
Tax at 22/40% pcm £584/£1062

TESTER'S NOTES
MATT PRIOR Funny how a soft-top can affect things. When it comes to coupés, I'd have a 911. Yet if the choice was a convertible, I'd have one of these over the Porsche every time. Cupholders are well back on the console, so elbows don't bash mugs.

JAMIE CORSTORPHINE Hood can be raised or lowered at speeds up to 30mph – helpful if the lights change. Glovebox is tiny – only enough for the leather-trimmed manual and a pair of gloves.

JOBS FOR THE FACELIFT
- More torque and more power: Vantage sounds the business but it's not always quick enough.
- Update the sat-nav system: needs better menu system and classier graphics.
- Make the clutch lighter.
- Make the dashboard buttons less fiddly.
- Don't touch the looks – it looks fine the way it is.

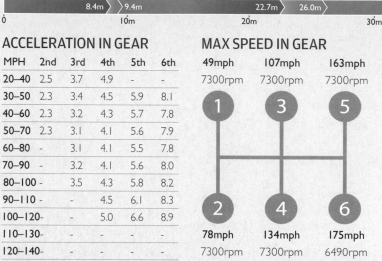

Start **T1** **T7** **T6** **T2** **T4** **T5** **T3** **DRY CIRCUIT**

ROADSTER v COUPÉ
Aston Martin V8 Roadster Lap Time 1.18.92 **dry and cloudy, 15°C**
Aston Martin V8 Coupé Lap Time 1.18.00 **dry and cloudy, 9°C**

Nearly as fast as the coupé here; revised suspension proves its worth. Brakes stand up to track use well despite increased kerb weight and, well, it sounds awesome.

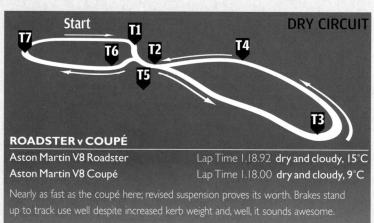

T2 **T3** **T1** **T4** **T5** **T6** **T8** **T7** **Start** **WET CIRCUIT**

ROADSTER v COUPÉ
Aston Martin V8 Roadster Lap time 1.10.02
Aston Martin V8 Coupé Lap time 1.8.78

Perhaps the stiffer front springs make a difference here. The Roadster failed to cut through the standing water and find front-end grip like the slightly softer coupé could.

Dials are modelled on top-end jewelled watches. They look great (especially when illuminated), but it can be difficult to read low speeds

Manual gearbox better now with a change in oil spec. It's still mechanical, just not such hard work

included additional strengthening, but the extent is minimal and it adds just 14kg to the chassis weight.

Other than the new fabric roof, which raises and lowers at the touch of a button in 22 seconds, and the addition of a pair of elegant buttresses to the rear deck, the roadster's design and construction mirrors that of the coupé with aluminium, steel and composite body panels.

The suspension architecture is also identical: aluminium double wishbones, coils springs and anti-roll bars front and rear. However, for the roadster Aston has tweaked the V8 Vantage set-up, increasing spring stiffness and raising the ride height – changes that will find their way into the coupé. Although our test car is a conventional six-speed manual, the roadster can be specifed with Sportshift (£3000), an automated manual with an electro-hydraulic clutch and steering wheel paddles.

INTERIOR ★★★★

Simply stepping inside the V8 Vantage's cabin goes a long way to conveying the magic of Aston Martin. The doors are hinged so that as they open they arch not just outwards but also upwards, and pulling them

shut behind you gives the impression of a closing canopy, leaving you encased in a cabin trimmed in soft leather, hand stitched – in the case of our test car – in contrasting yellow.

The seats, uprated from those fitted to the original Vantage coupé (new design and more lumbar adjustability) are low-set. With eight-way electric adjustment they can be arranged with a conventional flat base or, should you wish, a more sporting, Italian supercar, 'bum low, knees high' position. Either way, most sizes should be able to get comfortable behind the wheel.

BELOW Alcantara-lined cloth roof takes 22sec to open or close in a one-touch operation.

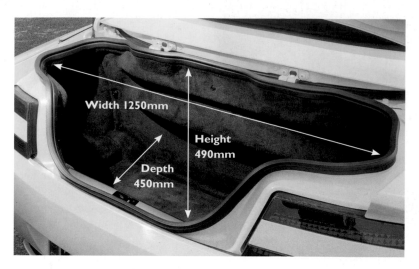

Width 1250mm

Height 490mm

Depth 450mm

ABOVE Boot can hold two sets of golf clubs on top of each other.

OPPOSITE Twin exhausts are integrated into the rear bodyshell. Exhaust system houses a bypass valve to ensure the Vantage meets drive-by noise regulations.

Your view is dominated by a high-set scuttle, sculpted into a curved wall of leather and dissected by a centre stack of controls for the heating, entertainment and optional navigation screen. The switchgear is a mixture of bespoke Aston Martin and parts borrowed from Volvo, but the combination is elegant and the design, for the most part, is ergonomically effective.

As with the Vantage coupé and the DB9 before it, the dials are worthy of particular praise, combining clarity with an alluring jewel-like appearance. They're

at their very best back-illuminated in the evening twilight. The inside of the roof is trimmed in tactile alcantara, blending neatly with the covering on the A-pillars, and it makes the soft-top feel no less sumptuous than the coupé.

Furthermore, the removable roof means little sacrifice on longer journeys; there is, as you'd expect, more wind noise than the tin-top, particularly around the B-pillars, but not so much to merit a disturbance.

The biggest price is more restricted rear three-quarter visibility, but that problem can easily be solved by lowering the roof, leaving a rear view interrupted only by the handsome buttresses.

Yet for all the Vantage roadster's glamour, it is not without its frustrations: some controls require a precise digit, the switches for the interior lights are confusingly jumbled in among the radio controls and there is precious little storage space in the cabin, while the boot is half the size of the coupé's (144 litres versus 300).

PERFORMANCE ★★★☆

The similarities between the coupé and the drop-top don't stop at their chassis. The V8 roadster also shares the coupé's 4.3-litre, dry-sumped V8 in precisely the same state of tune.

INSTANT GROUP TEST THE WORLD'S FINEST CONVERTIBLES COMPARED

MAKE	ASTON MARTIN	JAGUAR	PORSCHE	MERCEDES-BENZ
Model	**V8 Vantage roadster**	**XKR convertible**	**Carrera S cabriolet**	**SL55 AMG**
Price	£91,000	£73,495	£74,910	£99,885
Power	380bhp at 7000rpm	410bhp at 6250rpm	355bhp at 6600rpm	517bhp at 6100rpm
Torque	302lb ft at 5000rpm	413lb ft at 4000rpm	295lb ft at 4600rpm	531lb ft at 2600rpm
0–60mph	5.2sec	5.3sec (claimed)	4.9sec (claimed to 62mph)	4.5sec (claimed)
Top speed	175mph	155mph (claimed)	182mph (claimed)	155mph (claimed)
Fuel consumption	17.5mpg (18.8 combined)	22.3mpg (combined)	24.4mpg (combined)	20.9mpg (combined)
Kerbweight	1713kg	1715kg (claimed)	1505kg (claimed)	1960kg (claimed)
CO_2/tax band	358g/km, 35 per cent	294g/km, 35 per cent	280g/km, 35 per cent	324g/km, 35 per cent
We think	Looks sensational, entertaining handling and great noise. Pricey.	Excellent cruiser with slick proper auto and cosseting ride.	To take the roof off a 911 is dubious, but it is still the best drive here.	Brutal supercharged urge, slick auto and the security of a metal top.
VERDICT	★★★★	★★★★	★★★★☆	★★★★☆

So despite giving away 80kg to the coupé, the roadster has a broadly similar, junior-supercar level of performance. Aston claims the two are equally quick – at 4.9sec to 60mph and 175mph flat out – but we found different. We eventually persuaded the V8 Vantage to hit 60mph in under five seconds, but the roadster could only be coaxed to an average of 5.2sec.

With a higher drag coefficient (0.35 versus 0.34) and barely a difference in their frontal profiles, the roadster was also a tad slower on high-speed runs at Bruntingthorpe airfield, hitting 157mph compared with the coupé's 165mph in the same length of track.

But it's the nature of the naturally aspirated V8's power delivery that makes the Vantage roadster feel, if not exactly slow, then certainly more lethargic than most of its rivals. A Porsche 911 S cabriolet feels more responsive through more of its rev range than the Aston, while a Mercedes-Benz SL55 AMG feels positively ballistic in comparison.

The V8 Vantage's power delivery and response are soft at low revs, and it only offers real urgency above 4000rpm. Peak power (380bhp) doesn't arrive until 7000rpm, and peak torque (302lb ft) at 5000rpm.

WHAT IT COSTS

V8 VANTAGE ROADSTER

On-the-road price	£91,000
Price as tested	£97,995
Retained value 3yrs	£55,625
Typical PCP pcm	na
Contract hire pcm	na
Cost per mile	na
Insurance/typical quote	20/POA

EQUIPMENT CHECKLIST

Dynamic Stability Control	■
Electric front seats	■
Rear parking sensors	■
Alarm upgrade	**£195**
Leather upholstery	■
Memory seats	**£295**
Climate control	■
Steering reach/rake adj	■
Fine stitching	**£145**
160W stereo with 6-CD	■
18in alloy wheels	■

Cruise control	**£295**
Power fold wing mirrors	**£295**
19in 7-spoke alloys	**£995**
Satellite navigation	**£1750**
Heated seats	**£295**
Tyre pressure monitor	■
Sunburst yellow paint	**£995**
Xenon headlamps	**£495**
AM premium audio	**£995**
Wind deflector	**£395**
Black brake calipers	**£295**

Options in **bold** fitted to test car

■ = Standard na = not available

RANGE AT A GLANCE

ENGINES

4.3 V8	380bhp	£82,800
4.3 V8 Roadster	380bhp	£91,000

TRANSMISSIONS

Six-speed manual	std
Six-speed sportshift	£3000

SPECIFICATIONS V8 ROADSTER

DIMENSIONS

Front track 1570mm **Rear track** 1560mm **Width including mirrors** 2025mm
Width excluding mirrors 1865mm **Front interior width** 1385mm

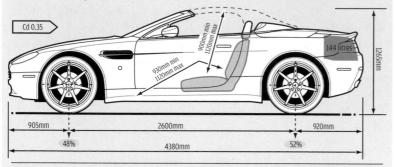

ENGINE

Installation	Front, longitudinal
Type	8 cyls in vee,
	4300cc, petrol
Made of	Alloy head & block
Bore/stroke	89.0/86.0mm
Compression ratio	11.3:1
Valve gear	4 per cyl
Power	380bhp at 7000rpm*
Torque	302lb ft at 5000rpm*
Red line	7300rpm
Power to weight	222bhp per tonne
Torque to weight	177lb ft per tonne
Specific output	88bhp per litre

TRANSMISSION

Gearbox 6-speed manual
Ratios/mph per 1000rpm
Final drive ratio 3.91

1st 3.15/6.4		2nd 1.97/10.3	
3rd 1.44/14.1		4th 1.15/17.6	
5th 0.94/21.6		6th 0.78/26.0	

CHASSIS AND BODY

Construction	Bonded aluminium structure
Weight/as tested	1710kg/1713kg
Drag coefficient	0.35
Wheels	8.5Jx19 (f), 9Jx19 (r), alloy
Tyres	235/40 ZR19 (f)
	275/35 ZR19 (r)
Spare	Foam kit

STEERING

Type Rack and pinion, hydraulic speed-dependent assistance
Turns lock-to-lock 3.0
Turning circle 11.1m

SUSPENSION

Front Double wishbones, coil springs, anti-roll bar
Rear Double wishbones, coil springs, anti-roll bar

BRAKES

Front 355mm ventilated, grooved discs
Rear 330mm ventilated, grooved discs
Anti-lock Standard, ESP, brake assist

At least when the V8 finally does let loose, it does so with a glorious, hard-edged V8 noise that hood-down driving lets you get the most from. If someone said this was the best engine note in production, we'd find it difficult to argue otherwise. But the truth is that at the other side of £90,000, the V8 roadster ought to feel seriously fast, and it doesn't.

We've no complaints about the brakes, though; they have a solid, progressive pedal feel and offer excellent stopping distances, wet or dry. They resist fade strongly, too.

RIDE AND HANDLING ★★★★

Although we criticised the V8 Vantage coupé for being less of a driver's car than, say, a Porsche 911, it seems harsh to say the same thing this time around. This is a convertible, after all, and the less frenetic dynamic make-up of the Aston actually suits the role of a drop-top rather well.

Removing the roof from the coupé has reduced the chassis' torsional rigidity by 18 per cent, but while you can feel it wobble ever so slightly over the worst road surfaces, the coupé's core driving characteristics are still there. This is a fundamentally well balanced sports car, albeit not the sharpest drive in the class.

But despite a loss of torsional stiffness, the roadster's suspension is actually stiffer than the coupé's. Front springs are 14 per cent stiffer, and the rears 16 per cent; the coupé will soon adopt these changes too.

Unsurprisingly, then, the roadster is a car that is better at controlling body movements than absorbing lumps and potholes, but it is comfortable enough for long-distance journeys.

The beefy qualities of the coupé's controls are still present and correct. The clutch is heavy and the gearshift hefty, with a long, occasionally obstructive throw. The steering is weighty and, at 3.1 turns lock to lock, relatively slow. But don't mistake the steering's heft for feel; it's linearly responsive, but there's less fluidity to it than there is in the coupé.

The roadster's handling stance backs up the beef that its controls suggest it will have. This is not an agile, pointy sports car.

Instead of it being lively and adjustable in corners, the roadster feels solid and stable. It takes quite a turn of the wheel before it settles into a turn, but once on line it holds on staunchly and resolutely before gently and controllably nudging into understeer. In the dry, it takes serious provocation to unsettle the V8 roadster from here. In the wet its line can more easily be adjusted on the throttle and it oversteers controllably, but the stiffer springs stop it from gripping so tenaciously in the first place.

BUYING AND OWNING ★★★

Costing £91,000 even in its most basic, manual trim (and that eye-watering figure could easily spill into six figures if you are tempted by the options list), the V8 Vantage roadster is far from good value, especially next to Jaguar's cheaper and more powerful XKR.

Yet to look at, to be seen in and to drive, we can understand that for some the justification will be easy. The Vantage produces a hefty 358g/km of CO_2 and, in our experience, averages just 17.5mpg, but it will hold its value like nothing else in this class.

LEFT Low-set seats are improved over those of coupé, with more lumbar support; Leather buttresses are another beautiful touch, helping to break up the flat rear deck and housing the pop-up roll bars.

SOFTLY SMOKIN'

DBS Aston Martin's DBS is the new Vanquish, so you'd expect a brutal, extreme range-topper. But, as Chris Harris discovers, it's a different beast entirely

There was a boy at my school whose voice did not belong to his body. It was a strange affliction. He was one of those oversize creatures who bypassed adolescence, instead moving straight from being a child to a man. Aged 15, he was a hulk of muscle. But his butch persona fell apart when he spoke, because from within this mammoth frame came the mildest of voices. And the threat of a beating never carried the same sense of gravity when it was delivered in tones more suited to a porcelain explanation on the *Antiques Roadshow*.

I do hope this softly spoken, modern-day Flashman has ended up being exceedingly wealthy, because I have just driven a car whose character squares so perfectly with his disposition that he should buy one immediately. It's called the new Aston Martin DBS, it costs £160,000, and it is one of the strangest cars I've stumbled across in a while.

We've known about the DBS for many, many moons. This knowledge and familiarity is perhaps the root cause of my confusion, because despite some initial concerns over potential crowding within the Aston range, I had recently begun to understand it. The stunning little V8 Vantage was the volume-chaser, the DB9 served a more mature audience and the Vanquish, the old soldier, remained the premium product. That last definition will remain pertinent to an understanding of the DBS.

The DBS replaces the Vanquish. It is the new super-Aston, the car that crowns a range whose slowest member can touch 180mph. Its styling certainly propounds just that message. When stationary, the DBS has the look of the tethered dog that would certainly inflict a flesh injury, but for the protective rope. It has 398mm carbon ceramic brake discs up front and slightly smaller dinner plates at the rear. It has adjustable Bilstein dampers and large areas of carbon fibre bodywork, and the optional fixed-back bucket seats looks suspiciously like they were modelled on the front chairs of a Porsche 964 RS. That's right: the DBS, with its front splitters and rear diffuser,

FIRST DRIVE

24 OCTOBER 2007

Volume 254

No 4 | 5764

ABOVE Restyled cabin looks overwrought and is less usable than that of DB9.

positively shouts the language of sports car at anyone within hearing distance.

Ten minutes after our introduction, rumbling out onto some open French N-roads, the confusion begins. This car has ride comfort. With the dampers set to soft, it is not just supple within the remit of a sports car; it is plain comfortable.

Over surfaces that would have any other current Aston fidgeting, the DBS glides. Its reactive dampers offer the driver two options – sport or comfort – and in each of those settings are programmed five separate damper characteristics. From those five, the computer aims to keep the car either as comfortable as possible in the comfort mode, or control any body movements as fast as possible in the sport mode. It sounds complicated, and it is complicated, but the upshot isn't quite what you'd expect. Because even with the dampers set to firm, this car still has 20 per cent more ride comfort than a Ferrari 599 GTB.

Aston has also relaxed its obsession with needlessly heavy steering. The power assistance has been altered, and the rack still operates through three turns of lock, but it still isn't anything like as incisive as rival machines

from Porsche and Ferrari. However, it is accurate enough to allow this 1695kg lump to be threaded with confidence along fairly narrow roads.

The limited-slip differential has been revised under power and on overrun, and it certainly has a marked effect on the handling; even small alterations in throttle push or pull the DBS's nose in turns.

And so where is the confusion? It lies in the chasm that exists between the visual promise and the driving characteristics. The DBS looks pugnacious – like it should never have been granted an exit from the Nürburgring – and yet to drive it is more comfortable than a DB9. It has lighter steering – in fact, the whole car is less demanding to drive – and despite now having 510bhp at 6500rpm and 420lb ft at what would appear to be a high 5750rpm, this car has the laziest performance of any Aston. Including those bonkers supercharged Vantages from the '90s. It is not a car that especially likes being hurried. It's the school hard man with the *Antiques Roadshow* voice.

Push the DBS and the rear axle doesn't feel especially well located and the steering column will flex slightly. Make a demand and the car will respond, but

the car more comfortable is both brave and realistic. This was never going to be a track car, so the fact that the 20in Pirelli P Zero Nero tyres are hushed at speed, the fact that the cabin is isolated from the outside world very effectively, and the fact that Aston told us it was going to build a super-coupé and has delivered a competent GT instead don't constitute a problem for me.

As something to cover ground, to use as a road car, it's a stunning machine. The motor sounds expensive (and it isn't hampered by quite the same level of silly exhaust noise as other Astons). It also has so much torque from 1800rpm that you'd swear some kind of forced induction was at work. And despite some harshness between 4500 and 5500rpm, it revs right out to the limiter. But oddly enough, it's the transmission – an old-school, six-speed Graziano manual with a clean shift action that doesn't really like being hurried – that gives the best insight into the type of car the DBS is.

The brakes deserve to be singled out. They have the best pedal feel of any ceramics I've ever driven, especially at low speeds, and not once during hours of hard use did they even grumble. Their contribution to the car's excellent comfort, given that they cut 5kg of unsprung mass at each corner, should not be underestimated, either.

LEFT Optional fixed-back buckets are even better than standard chairs. Engine starter is far too fiddly to make sense.

there's a hesitation as something takes up the slack in the chassis. It's as if everything you expected to be rose-jointed is in fact connected with rubber bushes.

How much this taints your view of the DBS is almost certainly bound up in your own personal view on the styling. Mine is not to decide what other people think constitutes a pretty car, but there are two irrefutable observations to be made about the DBS's looks. One is that the DB9 on which it is based has a cleaner shape.

The second runs along the same theme, but needs closer examination. Aston wants £160k for the DBS, a car which, to my eyes at least, looks like a spruced and preened DB9. Whether you think it better looking or not, Aston's decision to not give its flagship model a completely different set of clothes is a dangerous one. The other two model lines each have a clear identity, but the DBS is a derivative. People buying the most expensive model in the range should not be paying for derivative styling.

This need to differentiate the DBS from the DB9 pervades all aspects of the car, and some of the work has been very successful. I think the decision to make

A CAR THAT BEGS TO DIFFER

The maximum number of models from the minimum number of parts is the mantra of virtually all car manufacturers. Aston Martin is no different, so it's no surprise that the DBS is a development of the DB9.

All of Aston's new models are based on the aluminium VH1 chassis. And all the tricks in the book are used to make the DBS stand out on its own. It's lower, has wider tracks and rolls on larger wheels. A deeper front bumper, redesigned bonnet, sill extensions and modified wings signal just how far the DBS is from its tamer sister. Under the paint lurk carbon fibre panels.

Upgraded cabin materials, a new centre console spattered in turned alloy and lightweight bucket seats again give a new-model impression for a relatively small investment. The engine gets extra zest at the top of the rev range, and upgraded adaptively damped suspension and a de-bushed rear suspension subframe give the car a different edge than the DB9.

SUPER-COUPÉ CLASH

MAKE	ASTON MARTIN	FERRARI
Model	**DBS**	**599 gtb F1**
Price	£160,000	£184,902
0–60mph	4.1sec	3.7sec
0–100mph	9.3sec	7.4sec
Top speed	191mph	205mph
Power	510bhp at 6500rpm	611bhp at 6800rpm
Torque	420lb ft at 5750rpm	448lb ft at 5600rpm
Power to weight	300bhp per tonne	326bhp per tonne
Engine	V12, 5999cc, petrol	V12, 5935cc, petrol
Installation	Front, longitudinal, rwd	Front, longitudinal, rwd
Gearbox	6-spd manual	6-spd automated manual
Length	4721mm	4665mm
Width	1905mm	1962mm
Height	1280mm	1336mm
Wheelbase	2740mm	2750mm
Weight	1695kg	1695kg
Fuel tank	78 litres	105 litres
Tyres	245/35 R20 (f)	245/40 R20 (f)
	295/30 R20 (r)	305/35 R20 (r)

If the need to modify the DB9 underpinnings has perhaps finally released the platform's full grand touring potential, then the same cannot be said of the cabin. The DBS suffers at the hand of complication. It has its own centre console, which is both cluttered with tiny buttons and, in piano wood, looks suspiciously like that of an RX-8.

The gear lever is a preposterous lump of metal that only Andrew Sheridan could call wieldy and the start system is unfathomable. It's called ECU (Emotional Control Unit – geddit?), and you have to endure the vaguely Freudian weirdness of plunging a key-ish thing into a dash orifice with your index finger. If you don't get the clutch-down-and-insert sequence correct, you must remove and replunge. It drove me quite insane because it was endemic of a cabin where just about every instrument has been tweaked for reasons of fashion. At the expense of usability.

Turn the ignition on (if you can) and the dash winks the brand message 'Power, Beauty, Soul' at you each time. Turn on the hi-fi and the DBS logo lingers for a while. Everywhere is ostentation and obfuscation; the silver-faced dials have slightly revised fonts, but I still can't read them, and the rev counter that counter-rotates against the speedometer may look funky, but it doesn't help the driver. Too much funking up has been allowed here. People have got carried away – and the end result is a place that neither looks becoming of a £160k car, nor fits with the restrained Aston design message that has attracted so many new customers.

RIGHT Carbon fibre rear diffuser, which draws air out from the flat undertray.

OPPOSITE DBS is a hugely accomplished GT but lacks the majesty of the Vanquish; DBS's 510bhp 6.0-litre V12 sounds like a thoroughbred and has torque to spare.

If you can square the looks with the comfort-biased performance, the DBS still warrants serious consideration, because as an everyday road car it is some machine. But this is a tangential shift for Aston, and not one that fills me with hope for the future.

There was a singularity of style and purpose about the DB9 and the V8 Vantage when they were launched that gave them a distinct personality. The same cannot be said of the DBS. In being lighter, more accelerative and a much more accomplished grand tourer than the Vanquish S, the DBS is a fitting dynamic successor. But as a range figurehead, as a car whose very presence would inspire a V8 Vantage owner to graduate to the most expensive product, it does not have the same success.

There was a majesty about the Vanquish, almost all of it bound up in the fact that despite its pretty underlings, it still looked like the alpha male of the range. And that is missing in this car.

ASTON MARTIN DBS

Is the latest new model from Aston Martin a worthy replacement for the Vanquish, or a fettled DB9?

Taken at face value, the Aston Martin DBS is a strange kind of supercar flagship. Slower and less powerful than the Vanquish S of old and demonstrably a development of the DB9, after so many bold statements from the rejuvenated marque it appears as something of a pulled punch.

Or maybe not. Perhaps Aston Martin is, in fact, being very canny, because by positioning the DBS below the level of the likes of the Ferrari 599 and Lamborghini Murciélago yet above any Porsche, it has found some clear air for the DBS to breathe.

Even so, it is perhaps odd that Aston Martin has chosen to make so little visual differentiation between it and its little brother; there are extra louvres and slats, but the overall effect is still that of a DB9 to which too much make-up has been too hurriedly applied.

But Aston says itself that its construction was defined by "the need for high-performance stability, handling ability and low kerb weight", and if that is the form it requires to let it function at a level beyond that of any of the brand's previous models, then we have no quarrel with it.

DESIGN AND ENGINEERING ★★★☆

The DBS inherits both its bonded aluminium chassis and its 6.0-litre V12 from the DB9 but tunes both to

QUICK FACTS

Model tested	DBS
Price	£160,000
Power	510bhp
Torque	420lb ft
0–60mph	4.2sec
Fuel economy	15.1mpg
CO_2 emissions	388g/km
70–0mph	44.7m
Skidpan	1.03g

ROAD TEST

13 FEBRUARY 2008

Volume 255

No 7 | 5779

ABOVE DBS can crack 100mph in just 8.7sec, putting old Vanquish in the shade.

OPPOSITE Headlights look pretty but they offer startlingly little light for a car with this performance potential; thankfully, the substantial rear spoiler has been properly integrated into the bootlid, rather than tacked on like a cheap aftermarket addition.

HISTORY

The original DBS was introduced in 1967 as a supplemental model to the DB6, but continued in production until 1972, two years after the DB6's demise. Using a 4.0-litre straight six engine, it came with 282bhp in standard form, but with 325bhp as a Vantage. The original DBS starred in *On Her Majesty's Secret Service* and is in the car in which Tracy di Vicenzo, aka Mrs Bond, is shot dead by Irma Bunt. The current DBS was announced in 2006 and made its Bond debut in 2007, in *Casino Royale*.

suit its more extreme ends. The engine gains a bypass in its inlet port to allow it to breathe more easily at high revs, while the ports themselves have been reshaped to improve the flow of air into the engine. The result is a substantial power increase, from 450bhp at 6000rpm to 510bhp at 6500rpm. Peak torque remains unchanged at 420lb ft, but it comes in at 5750rpm rather than 5000rpm. Then again, carbon panels and ceramic brakes have dropped the kerb weight of the DBS by a claimed 65kg relative to the DB9, so there is less work for that torque to do.

The chassis has also been substantially revised. It benefits not only from bespoke spring and anti-roll bar settings but also a wider track and, most importantly, adaptive dampers that are capable of switching automatically between five different settings in the car's sport and comfort modes.

The brakes are not just carbon ceramic rather than steel; they're also colossal (398mm in diameter at the front compared with just 355mm on a DB9). No wonder you have to have 20in wheel rims on your DBS, in place of the standard 19in items on the DB9.

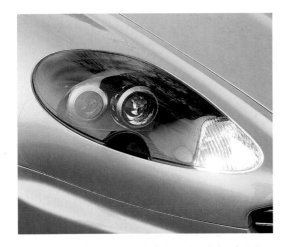

UNDER THE SKIN THE CARBON DIET

The DBS is the first Aston Martin road car to make extensive use of carbonfibre in its construction, and it uses techniques learned in the design and build of the DBR9 and DBRS9 GT racing cars.

But while the racers are clad entirely in carbon panels, the DBS makes use of the expensive but strong, lightweight material for the boot, front wings, bonnet and door opening surrounds. Aston Martin claims that these panels alone allow the DBS to weigh 30kg less than it would with equivalent aluminium items.

Carbon is also a crucial component of the ceramic brake system, which not only imbues the DBS with massive stopping power, but also reduces unsprung weight by a substantial 12.5kg.

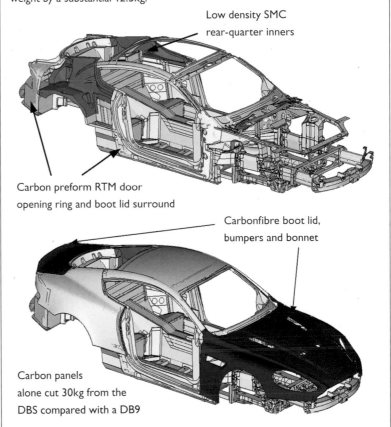

Low density SMC rear-quarter inners

Carbon preform RTM door opening ring and boot lid surround

Carbonfibre boot lid, bumpers and bonnet

Carbon panels alone cut 30kg from the DBS compared with a DB9

INTERIOR ★★★☆

Aston Martin takes a very particular approach with its interiors that will probably enthuse and infuriate in equal measure, depending on the priorities of its occupants. Those who like things on the showy side will be in heaven, for there is plenty of automotive jewellery in here. But those more interested in how things work are likely to put their blood pressure in the danger zone the moment they try even a simple task like setting a destination on the dreadful, ancient sat-nav system.

The centre console is a myriad of buttons, many of which are concealed behind the huge, ugly gear lever, and while acclimatisation will eventually familiarise you with their operation, we suspect you'd be in your grave before it became remotely intuitive.

That said, the driving position is excellent and the illegible dials are less of a problem than you might imagine, thanks to a large digital speedo and change-up lights that remove the need to use the rev counter. The steering wheel, which adjusts for rake and reach, is of the correct diameter for such

ROAD TEST ASTON MARTIN DBS

ACCELERATION Dry track, 9°C.

30mph	40	50	60	70	80	90	100	110	120	130	140	150		160
1.9s	2.5s	3.4s	4.2s	5.1s	6.4s	7.5s	8.7s	10.3s	12.0s	14.7s	17.3s	20.3s		23.9s

0 — 5s — 10s — 15s — 20s — 25s

DRY/WET BRAKING 60–0mph 2.81sec

	30mph-0	30mph-0		50mph-0	50mph-0		Dry 70mph-0	Wet 70mph-0
	8.3m	8.6m		22.6m	23.9m		44.7m	50.2m

0 — 10m — 20m — 30m — 40m — 50m

ACCELERATION IN GEAR

MPH	2nd	3rd	4th	5th	6th
20–40	1.9	2.6	3.3	-	-
30–50	1.8	2.6	3.2	4.1	5.5
40–60	1.8	2.5	3.2	4.1	5.4
50–70	1.7	2.5	3.2	4.1	5.5
60–80	-	2.4	3.2	4.2	5.7
70–90	-	2.4	3.1	4.2	5.9
80–100	-	2.5	3.1	4.3	6.0
90–110	-	-	3.2	4.4	6.3
100–120	-	-	3.3	4.5	6.6
110–130	-	-	-	4.7	7.1
120–140	-	-	-	5.0	7.7
130–150	-	-	-	5.6	8.5

MAX SPEED IN GEAR

47mph	102mph	157mph
6800rpm	6800rpm	6800rpm

① ③ ⑤

② ④ ⑥

76mph	128mph	194mph
6800rpm	6800rpm	6800rpm

ECONOMY

	TEST		CLAIMED
Average	15.1mpg	Urban	11.6mpg
Touring	18.0mpg	Ex-urb	24.1mpg
Track	6.5mpg	Comb	17.3mpg
Tank size	78 litres	Test range	260 miles

CABIN NOISE

Idle 51dB Max revs in 3rd 81dB 30mph 67dB
50mph 71dB 70mph 76dB

SAFETY

ABS, EBD, EBA, DSC
EuroNCAP crash rating   na
Pedestrian rating   na

GREEN RATING

CO_2 emissions   388g/km
Tax at 22/40% pcm   na/na

TESTER'S NOTES

ANDREW FRANKEL Flush-mounted exterior door handles look good but freeze solid in very cold weather; they take a lot of working loose.

MATT PRIOR The stereo system with integral iPod attachment offers stunning musical clarity, but lacks a little low-down punch.

JAMIE CORSTORPHINE Despite being more potent, the DBS emits fewer CO_2/km than the DB9, as Aston tries to cut emissions model by model.

JOBS FOR THE FACELIFT

- Provide some automatic lights and wipers. This car costs £160,000, after all.
- Design a centre console that works; the current arrangement is simply too irritating.

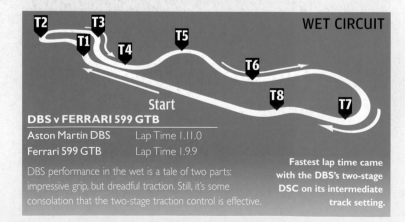

DRY CIRCUIT

DBS v FERRARI 599 GTB

Aston Martin DBS	Lap Time 1.13.3
Ferrari 599 GTB	Lap Time 1.12.7

DBS is at its best in dry conditions; it runs the 599 close, despite giving away more than 100bhp. Best results come with dampers set to sport.

Unlike the 599, which wanted to oversteer through T4, at the limit (touching 110mph) it's the DBS's nose that slips first.

WET CIRCUIT

DBS v FERRARI 599 GTB

Aston Martin DBS	Lap Time 1.11.0
Ferrari 599 GTB	Lap Time 1.9.9

DBS performance in the wet is a tale of two parts: impressive grip, but dreadful traction. Still, it's some consolation that the two-stage traction control is effective.

Fastest lap time came with the DBS's two-stage DSC on its intermediate track setting.

a car – albeit with a rim that's a smidge too thick and squishy for our tastes – and the weight of the pedals is perfectly judged, even if the throttle movement is slightly too long.

Behind the seats are two hollowed out shells where the DB9's rear seats have been removed, allowing Aston Martin to refer to the DBS (somewhat annoyingly) as a "2+0". Still, it's welcome extra luggage space to supplement a boot that's wide but not very long and rather shallow.

PERFORMANCE ★★★★☆

Look at the DBS and there is a temptation to view it as little more than a DB9 that's been dressed up for the most important job interview of its life. But that's a feeling that evaporates the moment you find your first open stretch of road and let the newly invigorated V12 do its stuff. Using Aston Martin's kerb weights, the DB9 has a power-to-weight ratio of 256bhp per tonne, while the DBS has over 300bhp per tonne, which means its carries the mark of an extremely serious performance car.

So read nothing into the fact that its 191mph top speed is just 4mph higher than that claimed for the

DB9, for that is purely a function of its additional downforce. Concentrate instead on the fact that despite the traction disadvantages of its front-engined, rear-drive configuration, the DBS flings itself to 100mph in 8.7sec, passing 60mph in 4.2sec on the way.

In stark contrast, the DB9 takes 11.3sec to make it into three figures. Even the old Vanquish pales

ABOVE Rear spoiler and carbon fibre diffuser define the rear view.

BELOW Boot is wide but quite short and shallow; space behind seats needs to be used.

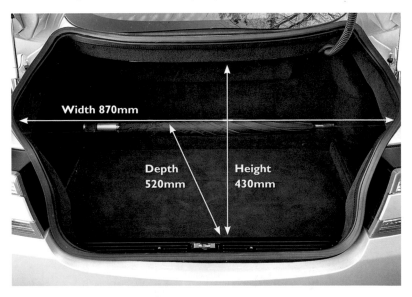

Width 870mm

Depth 520mm

Height 430mm

Key splits opinion. Some think it is genuinely desirable and others call it style over substance.

Dials are hard to read, but luckily the digital speedometer works well

INSTANT GROUP TEST

MAKE	FERRARI	LAMBORGHINI	ASTON MARTIN	ASTON MARTIN

Model	**599GTB**	**Murciélago LP640**	**DBS**	**DB9 Sport Pack**
Price	£197,300	£197,985	£160,000	£113,345
Power	611bhp at 7600rpm	631bhp at 8000rpm	510bhp at 6500rpm	450bhp at 6000rpm
Torque	448lb ft at 5600rpm	487lb ft at 6000rpm	420lb ft at 5750rpm	420lb ft at 5000rpm
0–60mph	3.7sec	3.5sec	4.2sec	4.7sec (claimed)
Top speed	205mph+ (claimed)	210mph (claimed)	191mph (claimed)	186mph (claimed)
Fuel consumption	11.8mpg (combined)	12.3mpg (combined)	15.1mpg (combined)	17.8mpg (comb/claimed)
Kerbweight	1690kg	1765kg	1730kg	1760kg (claimed)
CO_2/tax band	490g/km, 35 per cent	495g/km, 35 per cent	388g/km, 35 per cent	421g/km, 35 per cent
We think	Ferrari's finest is the most captivating front-engined road car on sale.	Last old-school supercar combines amazing pace with accessible handling.	Aston's best GT yet, but it struggles to shake off its DB9 roots.	DBS's baby sis is cheaper and prettier but not quite as good to drive.
VERDICT	★★★★★	★★★★½	★★★★	★★★★

by comparison, with its 4.6sec run to 60mph and 10.1sec needed to hit 100mph. Yes, both a Ferrari 599 GTB and Lamborghini Murciélago LP640 are capable of mid-three and sub-eight-second runs to 60mph and 100mph respectively, but it is not just their performance that's in a different league to the Aston; so are their prices.

And the Aston continues to delight when you look past such bald numbers. Despite its apparently sky-high torque peak, in fact there's solid urge available from as little as 2500rpm that just gently builds in urgency until peak power is reached 4000rpm further around the dial.

Better still, the V12 has never sounded better in its nine years powering Astons. Rich and sonorous in the mid-range, its voice evolves to an urgent, piercing howl as it nears its 6900rpm cut-off; every decibel is what you'd hope for in a 21st-century Aston Martin.

And while it will find its detractors, we are great fans of the simple six-speed gearbox. The linkage to the Graziano 'box slung between the rear wheels has been much improved since we first tried a manual DB9, and with a light and progressive clutch, a shortened final drive and a fast-yet-precise action across the gate, it is a decent gear lever away from providing a transmission perfectly suited to the DBS's character.

WHAT IT COSTS

ASTON MARTIN DBS		
On-the-road price	£160,000	
Price as tested	£160,195	
Value after 3yrs	na	
Typical PCP pcm	na	
Contract hire pcm	na	
Cost per mile	na	
Insurance/typical quote	20/£963	

EQUIPMENT CHECKLIST	
20-inch alloy wheels	■
Automatic climate control	■
Xenon Headlights	■
Trip computer	■
Leather/Alcantara seats	■/■
Electric/heated seats	■/■
Cruise control	■

Front/rear parking sensors	■/■
Front/side/curtain airbags	■/■/■
Keyless entry	■
Alarm upgrade	£195
MP3/iPod connection	■
HDD Satellite navigation	■
Bluetooth connectivity	■
700w premium audio system	■
Metallic paint	■

Options in **bold** fitted to test car

■ = Standard na = not available

RANGE AT A GLANCE

ENGINES		
6.0 V12	510bhp	£160,000

TRANSMISSIONS	
6-spd manual	std

RIDE AND HANDLING ★★★★

Subjective assessment suggests that, not for the first time, Aston has been tinkering with chassis specifications in the period between its original launch and providing us with a car for detailed

SPECIFICATIONS DBS

DIMENSIONS

Front track 1586mm Rear track 1581mm Width including mirrors 2060mm
Width excluding mirrors 1905mm Wheelbase 2740mm

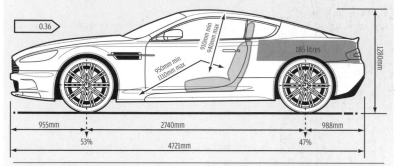

0.36

910mm min 940mm max
185 litres
1280mm
950mm min 1110mm max
955mm 2740mm 988mm
53% 47%
4721mm

ENGINE

510bhp at 6500 rpm
420lb ft at 5750 rpm

Installation	Front, longitudinal
Type	V12, 5935cc, petrol
Made of	Alloy head & block
Bore/stroke	89.0/79.5mm
Compression ratio	10.9:1
Valve gear	4 per cyl
Power	510bhp at 6500rpm
Torque	420lb ft at 5750rpm
Red line	6800rpm
Power to weight	301bhp per tonne
Torque to weight	248lb ft per tonne
Specific output	86bhp per litre

TRANSMISSION

Type	Rear-wheel drive
Gearbox	6-speed manual
Ratios/mph per 1000rpm	
Final drive ratio	3.71

1st 3.154/6.9	2nd 1.947/11.1
3rd 1.435/15.1	4th 1.148/18.8
5th 0.935/23.1	6th 0.758/28.5

CHASSIS AND BODY

Construction	Aluminium bonded tub
Weight/as tested	1695kg/1730kg
Drag coefficient	0.36
Wheels	20in, alloy
Tyres	245/35 ZR20 (f), 295/30 ZR20 (r) Pirelli P Zero
Spare	Repair kit
Safety	ABS, EBD, EBA, DSC

STEERING

Type	Hydraulically assisted rack and pinion
Turns lock-to-lock	3.0
Turning circle	12.0m

SUSPENSION

Front Double wishbones, coil springs, anti-roll bar, adaptive dampers
Rear Double wishbones, coil springs, anti-roll bar, adaptive dampers

BRAKES

Front 398mm ventilated carbon discs
Rear 360mm ventilated carbon discs
Anti-lock Standard, EBD, EBA

THE SMALL PRINT *Power- and torque-to-weight figures www.astonmartin.com. Cost-per-mile figures calculated over three years/36,000 miles, including depreciation and maintenance but not insurance; Lloyds TSB Autolease (0870 600 6333). Insurance quote covers 35-year-old professional male with clean licence and full no-claims bonus living in Swindon; from What Car? Insurance (0845 123 2618). Contract hire figure based on a three-year lease/36,000-mile contract including maintenance; from Lombard (0870 902 3311).

assessment. But while the DB9's chassis went backwards in this period, the DBS's has taken a substantial step forward and it is to be hoped that the car we drove is now representative of what will be delivered to customers. We shall certainly be borrowing one such car to find out.

But presuming that what you see is what you get, what lies beneath the DBS is a chassis that, in many areas, sets new standards for Aston Martin and approaches its very best rivals.

Most impressive is the new damper system. You can firm them up by pressing a button on the dash, whereupon the ride will deteriorate quite considerably, but left in normal comfort mode the DBS rides with a fluency we consider to be unrivalled in its class. Not only does it possess all the primary body control that any car of this performance potential needs, but it also

rear tyres in third gear, while if the road is wet the traction control light can become a constant companion. Even in the dry you cannot take for granted that it will transmit its power cleanly to the road in a way that even the more powerful 599 GTB can manage with ease.

BUYING AND OWNING ★★★★

We don't expect the DBS to be affected by the same levels of depreciation currently being seen in other Aston products thanks to the considerably lower numbers in which it will be built. And while its £160,000 list price might seem steep, it has to be remembered that this is a car with very few options to ramp the price up further, and it gets standard ceramic brakes that until recently were an £11,000 option on a Ferrari 599 GTB.

It's also less harmful to your wallet than we had anticipated. Although test procedures had the usual calamitous effect on fuel consumption, if you simply cruise down the motorway it will return a steady 18mpg, giving a usable range of almost 300 miles, despite the smallish 78-litre fuel tank.

Most impressive of all is the level of refinement Aston Martin has achieved. Road roar becomes oppressive only on very coarse surfaces, wind noise is well suppressed, and the big V12 is vocal when you want it to be and near silent the rest of the time. Given the excellence of its ride, it makes for a formidably able long-distance tourer.

obliterates all manner of small lumps and bumps that cause other supercars to jog and jiggle their way down the road.

It's true that the steering could do with more feel, but it remains very precise and perfectly weighted. And with three turns across its locks, it eschews the modern fashion of fitting very quick steering racks with the aim of making a car feel responsive but, more often than not, simply making it feel more nervous.

This translates into a car that is fabulously easy to drive. The body control is good enough at sane speeds for the car's considerable size not to be a problem, the steering ensures you hit every apex and the brilliant Brembo brakes are untaxed even by a car of this performance potential.

The only serious criticism concerns a lack of traction. On damp roads the DBS will spin its

AUTOCAR VERDICT

By putting such distance between it and the DB9 in price and name alike while mentioning it in the same breath as its Le Mans class-winning DBR9 racers, Aston Martin is making promises about the DBS that it has difficulty honouring at times. But none of this makes it a bad car or even, once you've figured it out, a disappointing one.

It is, if you like, the optimal DB9, a touring car that's been honed to have a sharper edge but whose natural environment remains the open road, not the mountain pass.

Calling this car the DB9S and charging £30,000 less for it would have reflected its positioning and abilities with much greater accuracy and resulted in a more positive outcome from this test. Even so, with time and miles it soon becomes clear that it is, in fact, Aston's greatest GT to date.

More DB9 than new Vanquish, but still a compelling grand tourer   ★★★★